THE RED SEA RULES

10 GOD-GIVEN STRATEGIES
FOR DIFFICULT TIMES

ROBERT J. MORGAN

THOMAS NELSON
Since 1798

NASHVILLE   DALLAS   MEXICO CITY   RIO DE JANEIRO   BEIJING

Published in Nashville, Tennessee, by Thomas Nelson, Inc.
Published in association with the literary agency of Alive Communications, 7680 Goddard Street, Suite 200, Colorado Springs, CO 80920.

For information on all translations used, see the notes section at the back of the book.

Library of Congress Cataloging-in-Publication Data

Morgan, Robert J., 1952–
    The Red Sea rules : 10 God-given strategies for difficult times / Robert J. Morgan.
        p. cm.
    ISBN 13: 978-0-7852-6649-5
    1. Bible. O.T. Exodus XIV—Criticism, interpretation, etc. 2. Christian life. I. Title.

    BS1245.2 .M67 2001
    248.4—dc21

                                                                                2001040335

Printed in the United States of America

11 12 13 14 WRZ 35 34 33 32

To Katrina

Contents

Preface

The Lord will make a way for you where no foot has been before.

That which, like a sea, threatens to drown you, shall be a highway for your escape.

—Charles H. Spurgeon

The Middle Eastern sun was down, the cold envelope of night having closed around Jerusalem. The streets of the old stone city were emptying as stragglers stumbled home. All over town, oil lamps yielded the last of their flickering lights and pungent odors, and embers lay dying in hearths.

But in a tiny room near the temple, a man named Asaph was awake, sitting blanket enfolded on the edge of a small bed. His world was in ruins, and though exhausted, he couldn't sleep.

Finally he lit his lamp and started reading his Bible. His mind recalled the miracle at the Red Sea, the story in Exodus 14 when the waters parted, allowing the children of Israel to escape the pursuing armies of Pharaoh.

Asaph later recorded his thoughts in Psalm 77 where,

after describing his anguish, he turned his thoughts to the power of God in days of old:

> You made a way through the sea
> and paths through the deep waters,
> but your footprints were not seen.
> You led your people like a flock
> by using Moses and Aaron. (Ps. 77:19–20 NCV)

In that story—in that God—Asaph found overcoming strength.

Just think of it: the winds blew, the sea split, the waters congealed into towering walls, and the Israelites passed through dry-shod. This happened not for the entertainment value of the experience, but to prove to us in earth-shaking, history-making fashion that, even when we are most anxious and distressed, God will make a way when there seems to be no way.

I, too, am an Asaph. Not long ago I was flying from Athens to New York, dealing with a problem that had reduced me to a bundle of nerves. Someone I loved was in trouble. Gazing down on the choppy Atlantic, I asked God for His help, then opened my Bible. The day's reading, as it happened, was Exodus 14.

The seat beside me was vacant, but as I began reading, I felt as though the Lord Himself were sitting beside me, tutoring me through the passage. My fingers reached for a pen, and I started scribbling.

As I worked through the chapter, ten rules unfolded like rubber life rafts; ten ways of handling dilemmas and discouragements—a divine protocol for handling life when we find ourselves caught between the devil and the deep Red Sea.

I spent the rest of the flight pondering my notes, and once home, I actively applied these principles to my problems. I found them then, as I've found them since, a powerful and effective strategy for coping with the messes and stresses of life.

These aren't ten quick-and-easy steps to instant solutions. In my case, it took quite a while to work through the anguish and achieve a positive result. However, like Asaph, I found that Exodus 14 provides a biblical method to process difficulties by faith, in the light of God's almighty presence, providence, promises, and power.

The Red Sea may roll before us; the desert may entrap us; the enemy may press on our heels. The past may seem implausible and the future impossible, but God works in ways we cannot see. He will make a way of escape for His weary, but waiting, children.

> *I [the Lord] will even make a way* in the wilderness, and rivers in the desert. (Isa. 43:19 KJV, emphasis added)

> When you pray, keep alert and be thankful. Be sure to pray that God *will make a way.* (Col. 4:2–3 CEV, emphasis added)

> The LORD will utterly . . . *make a way* to cross on foot. (Isa. 11:15 NRSV, emphasis added)

> You can trust God. He will not let you be tested more than you can stand. But when you are tested, He will also *make a way* out so that you can bear it. (1 Cor. 10:13 BECK)

No sea is deeper than the ocean of His love. There is no army stronger than His hosts, no force greater than His throne of grace, no enemy who can overcome His direct and indirect work in our lives.

The reality of the Red Sea, in a word, is this: God will always make a way for His tired, yet trusting, children, even if He must split the sea to do it.

RED SEA RULE 1

Realize that God means for you to be where you are.

Now the LORD spoke to Moses, saying: "Speak to the children of Israel, that they turn and camp before Pi Hahiroth, between Migdol and the sea, opposite Baal Zephon."

—EXODUS 14:1–2

Cul-de-Sacs

The sea was before them, Pharaoh's hosts behind them, and the mountains around them. And all this, be it observed, permitted and ordered of God.

—C. H. MACKINTOSH

Reba Robinson lay awake night after night, tense and tired in her little room in Starkville, Mississippi.[1] Her imagination raced out of control as her fingers clung to an old T-shirt that had once belonged to her son and still carried the scent of his cologne. He was confronting death in some exotic locale, though she didn't know where or what for, how or by whom.

Dillon was a marine assigned to a covert commando unit. His assignments were so secretive that even his mother could not be told the time or location of his missions.

But her mother's instincts told her when he was in harm's way, and during those times she fervently prayed for Dillon day and night. She was undoubtedly praying the night he swam ten miles from a submarine to the forbidden coast of a hostile country. She was praying the night he parachuted behind enemy lines from a high-flying aircraft. She was praying the day he jumped from a chopper through a hail of bullets, his eyes blinded with tears, to retrieve the body of his fallen compatriot. She was praying the night a terrorist stuck a gun in his face and pulled the trigger; and perhaps it was her prayers that caused the gun to jam, giving Dillon the split second he needed to "resolve the problem" and escape.

She prayed through nocturnal tears and terrors and torments.

When Dillon finally returned home, he was a hero whose bravery could never be explained, declassified, or honored. He couldn't discuss his exploits or seek help in processing his traumas. He tried making the transition from action hero to typical guy, but life slowed to a snail's pace in his little hometown. He began frequenting the local bars, trying not to remember what he couldn't forget.

Reba prayed on.

Like Dillon's mother, we sometimes go through prolonged periods of pain and pressure. Trapped by circumstances. Hurting. Afraid. Facing impossible odds. Traversing long, dark valleys.

Some circumstances are beyond our control, and something as simple as the ringing of a phone, a card in the mail, or a knock on the door can push us off the wire. We fall into a world of worry. Someone defined worry as a small trickle of fear that meanders through the mind, cutting a channel into which all other thoughts flow.

The preacher John R. Rice said, "Worry is putting question marks where God has put periods."

Bishop Fulton J. Sheen called worry "a form of atheism, for it betrays a lack of faith and trust in God."

But for some of us, worry seems as inherent as breathing.

We are, after all, likened in the Bible to sheep. I have a small flock of sheep (well, three of them) that live contentedly in our extended backyard. They're well fenced and well fed, and they have little to fear. But they sometimes fear anyway and can bolt in sheer panic at nothing more than a rabbit jumping through the grass.

That isn't a quality the Lord admires in His sheep. He wants us to say, "Though I walk through the valley of the shadow of death, I will fear no evil . . ."

Recently, the phone rang in the wee hours. It was my sister, Ann, telling me that Mother had fallen ill, and they were rushing her to the hospital, but with little hope. Ann suggested I return home immediately. It was a terrible jolt, and an awful dread swept over me. But instantly a verse of Scripture came to mind—Psalm 116:15: *Precious in the sight of the LORD is the death of His saints.* From that moment, the grip of panic fell away, and I had peace.

Yet at other times, fear doesn't release its tenacious grip so easily. How can you *not* worry, after all, when you have a commando son being secretly inserted into deadly situations around the globe?

How can you *not* worry when your outflow exceeds your income, and the creditors are calling? Or when your financial portfolio is collapsing?

How can you *not* worry when your loved one is diagnosed with cancer?

How can you *not* worry when your job is terminated, your child is troubled, or your safety is at stake?

To put it differently, how can you *not* worry when the Red Sea faces you, the desert surrounds you, and the soldiers of Egypt are speeding toward you with drawn swords?

Just ask Reba Robinson. When amid her anxiety she accepted that God had placed her in that situation, difficult as it was, she began converting her worries into prayers and her fears into faith. She earnestly prayed for her son, trusting God to intervene, to redeem, to help, and to heal.

At a critical juncture in Dillon's life, a friend invited him to a revival meeting in a nearby church. He went grudgingly, intending to bolt as soon as the service was over. But the message struck home that night, and when the altar call was given, Dillon gripped the back of the pew as if trying to choke it. No terrorist had ever pursued him like the Hound of heaven. He later admitted, "I had faced death without shaking, but that night I was trembling like a leaf."

He staggered to the altar in tears, and that night a muscular, unsung hero fell to his knees and received Jesus Christ as Lord and Savior.

In the story of the Red Sea, the Israelites followed the pillar of cloud and fire as carefully as possible, thrilled with their new freedom, full of excitement about the future. Yet as they followed Him, God deliberately led them into a cul-de-sac between hostile hills, to the edge of a sea too deep to be forded and too wide to be crossed.

The unmistakable implication of Exodus 14:1–2 is that the Lord took responsibility for leading them into peril. He gave them specific, step-by-step instructions, leading them down a route to apparent ruin: *Turn and camp. Camp there. There, before the entrapping sea. Yes, right there in that impossible place.*

The Lord occasionally does the same with us, testing our faith, leading us into hardship, teaching us wisdom, showing us His ways. Our first reaction may be a surge of panic and a sense of alarm, but we must learn to consult the Scriptures for guidance.

So, take a deep breath and recall this deeper secret of the Christian life: *when you are in a difficult place, realize that the Lord either placed you there or allowed you to be there, for reasons perhaps known for now only to Himself.*

The same God who led you *in* will lead you *out*.

When You Find Yourself . . .

"He knows the way He taketh," even if for the moment we
do not.

—J. I. PACKER

Our whole perspective changes when, finding ourselves
in a hard place, we realize the Lord has either placed us
there or allowed us to be there, perhaps for reasons
presently known only to Himself.

On their first wedding anniversary, August 18, 1938,
Russell and Darlene Deibler arrived in New Guinea to
labor in the jungles for Christ. When the Japanese invaded
the East Indies, the two were torn apart, and Russell was
interned in a concentration camp where he died.

Darlene was imprisoned in another military camp where
she suffered years of forced labor, indignity, near starvation,
and afflictions such as beriberi, dysentery, and intestinal
worms.

One day she was singled out for execution. Shock troops
took her to a death camp and directed her toward a stark
cell. These words were written on the door in chalk: *Orang*

ini musti mati, "This person must die." The guards shoved her in the cell, and as the door slammed shut, Darlene fell on her knees to peer through the keyhole. When she saw the key make a complete revolution, she knew she was as good as dead.

As the footsteps of the guard receded, she fell backward in a cold sweat, trembling, fighting off sheer terror. Just then she found herself singing a song she had learned as a child in Sunday school back in Iowa:

> Fear not, little flock,
> Whatever your lot;
> He enters all rooms,
> "The doors being shut."
> He never forsakes,
> He never is gone,
> So count on His presence
> In darkness and dawn.
> *("Only Believe" by Daniel Reader)*

Darlene felt strong arms about her, and she knew that though her captors could lock her in, they could not lock out her wonderful Lord. She was in an impossible spot, but she was there with a God who does impossible feats. She was there in His will, and she knew that His will would never put her where His presence could not sustain her.

That assurance bore her through impossible times and pre-served her life despite impossible odds.[2]

Consider these men and women who, through no fault of their own, found themselves beset with soul-disabling difficulties while trying to follow God:

Hagar, a single mom, was forced into the desert with her boy to die of thirst.

Joseph, wanting to fulfill divine dreams, was seized, stripped, sold as a slave, and imprisoned in Egypt.

Moses was caught between the splendors of Egyptian roy-alty and thankless affliction with God's people.

David, being anointed by Samuel, was pursued by Israelite troops.

Hezekiah, seeking revival, was trapped by the most pow-erful army on earth, bent on annihilating his people.

The Lord's disciples sailed at His command on Galilee only to face a terror-filled night of storms and waves.

The Son of man Himself, fulfilling the Father's will, was nailed fast to wood and left to hang by His hands until dead.

The apostles, trying to preach this Crucified One, were horsewhipped.

The leader of that apostolic band later told his readers: "Beloved, do not think it strange concerning the fiery trial which is to try you, as though some strange thing happened to you" (1 Peter 4:12).

In other words, Christians shouldn't be surprised when, in seeking to do God's will, we find ourselves trapped in painful, frightening, difficult, or impossible situations. Life is hard—especially for Christians. We have a determined enemy seeking to devour us. "In the world," Jesus warned, "you will have tribulation" (John 16:33).

Then He added: "But be of good cheer, I have overcome the world."

God allows our faith to be tried, and He permits troubles to crowd into our lives. Sometimes they seem more than we can bear, but Christ can bear them. The first step toward "parted waters" is to frequently remind ourselves that the Lord has either put us in this difficult place or has allowed us to be there for reasons perhaps only He knows.

I've often wondered why my wife developed multiple sclerosis just as our children were leaving the nest. We had hoped to spend the last half of our marriage enjoying long-anticipated activities, such as traveling or golfing, that are now becoming difficult or impossible. Her struggles create struggles of my own, and occasionally I'm tempted to ask *why?*

But God has a purpose, and as hymnist William Cowper (pronounced Cooper) put it, "God is His own interpreter, and He will make it plain."

Years ago, I found this untitled and unattributed poem in a little volume by V. Raymond Edman titled *The Disciplines of Life:*

> When God wants to drill a man,
> And thrill a man,
> And skill a man
> To play the noblest part;
> When He yearns with all His heart
> To create so great and bold a man
> That all the world shall be amazed,
> Watch His methods, watch His ways!
> How He ruthlessly perfects
> Whom He royally elects!
> How He hammers him and hurts him,
> And with mighty blows converts him
> Into trial shapes of clay which
> Only God understands;
> While his tortured heart is crying
> And he lifts beseeching hands!
> How He bends but never breaks
> When his good He undertakes;
> How He uses whom He chooses,

> And with every purpose fuses him;
> By every act induces him
> To try His splendor out—
> God knows what He's about.[3]

There are no mistakes in God's plan; Jesus does all things well. A. W. Tozer said, "To the child of God, there is no such thing as an accident. He travels an appointed way. . . . Accidents may indeed appear to befall him and misfortune stalk his way; but these evils will be so in appearance only and will seem evils only because we cannot read the secret script of God's hidden providence."[4]

This idea is summed up in an incident in the life of South African pastor Andrew Murray, who once faced a terrible crisis. Gathering himself into his study, he sat a long while quietly, prayerfully, thoughtfully. Presently his mind flew to his Lord Jesus. Picking up his pen, he wrote this in his journal:

> First, He brought me here, it is by His will that I am in this strait place: in that fact I will rest.
>
> Next, He will keep me here in His love, and give me grace to behave as His child.
>
> Then, He will make the trial a blessing, teaching me the lessons He intends me to learn, and working in me the grace He means to bestow.
>
> Last, in His good time He can bring me out again—how and when He knows.

Let me say I am here,
(1) By God's appointment,
(2) In His keeping,
(3) Under His training,
(4) For His time.

Have you witnessed God's power in the past? Experienced His pardon? Enjoyed His presence? He who has carried you this far isn't going to drop you now.

The steps of a good man are ordered by the LORD,
And He delights in his way.
Though he fall, he shall not be utterly cast down;
For the LORD upholds him. (Ps. 37:23–24)

He has promised never to leave you or forsake you, never to forget, never to abandon. His love never ceases, and His care never dims.

So if you find yourself in a difficult spot, remember: you are there by God's appointment, in His keeping, under His training, and for His time.

And all evidence to the contrary, there's no better place to be.

What If It's My Fault?

Our God is a God who not merely restores, but takes up our mistakes and follies into His plan for us and brings good out of them.

—J. I. PACKER

What if we have landed in this tough spot not because the Lord directly led us there, but because we followed our own noses? We sometimes cause our own pain. Our problems often result from sheer selfishness or stupidity. What then?

Serious and sincere repentance routes us back into God's will. Confession is like a shortcut from the wayward path back to the straight and narrow road of Christ. When we genuinely repent of our sins, they are cast as far from us as east from west. Our hearts are cleansed, and our fellowship with God is restored. Certain consequences may linger, but the Lord will somehow use even those for good. Healing will still be needed, but the Great Physician will apply the salve. He weaves everything together to advance His purposes.

God's forgiveness allows self-forgiveness. Have you

ever read what Joseph told his brothers long after they had sold him into slavery? "Stop beating yourselves up over this," he said.

Joseph declared, "Do not be distressed and do not be angry with yourselves for selling me here, because it was to save lives that God sent me ahead of you. . . . Don't be afraid. Am I in the place of God? You intended to harm me, but God intended it for good to accomplish what is now being done" (Gen. 45:5; 50:19–20 NIV).

Self-forgiveness comes when we realize that if God has forgiven us, we needn't remain angry with ourselves, needn't hate ourselves any longer. God will use it all for good. According to Romans 8:28, "All things go on working together for the good of those who keep on loving God, who are called in accordance with God's purpose" (WILLIAMS).

"There is a compassionate adaptability about God's will for us," observed Sidlow Baxter. "Because we have not been in God's special will for us from the beginning, there is no reason why we should not get into it now. He can take up from where we get right."

After genuine confession and repentance, we can start wherever we are with Red Sea Rule #1: remember that God, in His overruling providence, has allowed you to be where you are at this moment.

One older commentator of Exodus 14 said, "When God fixes our position for us, we may rest assured that it is a wise and salutary one; and even when we foolishly and willfully choose a position for ourselves, He most graciously over-rules our folly, and causes the influences of our self-chosen circumstances to work for our spiritual benefit."

Trust Him. He can still make a way.

Red Sea
Rule 2

Be more concerned
for God's glory than
for your relief.

Pharaoh will say of the children of Israel, "They are bewildered by the land; the wilderness has closed them in." Then I will harden Pharaoh's heart, so that he will pursue them; and I will gain honor over Pharaoh and over all his army, that the Egyptians may know that I am the LORD.

—EXODUS 14:3–4

Asking the Right Question

If we could only look upon a difficult crisis as an occasion of bringing out, on our behalf, the sufficiency of divine grace, it would enable us to preserve the balance of our souls and to glorify God, even in the deepest waters.

—C. H. MACKINTOSH

In 1946, author Gertrude Stein felt very tired and ill during a car journey. Rushed to the American hospital at Neuilly, France, she was diagnosed with an advanced state of cancer. The surgeon operated, but it was too late. Gertrude passed away on the evening of July 27. Her last words baffled those around her. "What is the answer?" she asked. When nobody replied, she laughed to herself and said, "In that case, what is the question?"

Sometimes we can't find the answers to our dilemmas because we're asking the wrong questions. Perhaps, like Gertrude Stein, we find ourselves diagnosed with an incurable disease. Or we have a child in crisis, or we are facing a complicated legal problem. Maybe the money isn't there for college, or we're in a difficult relationship. Perhaps we've been jilted by a girlfriend or boyfriend—or spouse. Our natural instinct is to ask:

"How did I get into this mess, and how can I get out?"

"How quickly can I solve this problem?"

"Why did this have to happen to me?"

These are natural questions, but they may be the wrong ones to ask. There is a better approach, one that results in an entirely new way of looking at difficulties, that puts our problems into a different context and creates a new paradigm for dealing with tough situations.

The next time you're overwhelmed, instead of asking, "How can I get out of this mess?" try asking, "How can God be glorified in this situation?" One's perspective is entirely changed by the spiritual realities behind that approach. It's like switching on floodlights in a dark stadium.

Notice the way this develops in Exodus 14:3–4: "Pharaoh will say of the children of Israel, 'They are bewildered by the land; the wilderness has closed them in.' Then I will harden Pharaoh's heart, so that he will pursue them; and I will gain honor over Pharaoh and over all his army, that the Egyptians may know that I am the LORD."

God deliberately orchestrated the Exodus events as an occasion for demonstrating the power He wields over both

His enemies and the elements. The New International Version puts it, "I will gain glory for myself through Pharaoh; and all his army."

On that dramatic evening, God's glory sparkled in the moonlight as the ocean's spray dashed and danced hither and yon until the waters divided and the sea floor appeared as dry ground. His honor rose up in liquid walls before the wide-eyed Israelites, and His exploits became the substance of their songs and stories for a thousand generations.

You, too, can view your problem as an occasion for God to work wonders. Consider the words of Psalm 136:

> Oh, give thanks to the LORD, for He is good!
>> For His mercy endures forever . . .
> To Him who alone does great wonders,
>> For His mercy endures forever . . .
> To Him who divided the Red Sea in two,
>> For His mercy endures forever . . .
> But overthrew Pharaoh and his army in the Red Sea,
>> For His mercy endures forever.

Wax in the Sunshine

*I know He tries me only to increase my faith, and that is all
in love. Well, if He is glorified, I am content.*

—J. HUDSON TAYLOR

The Lord Jesus Himself practiced Red Sea Rule #2 when
difficulties and demands complicated His agenda. In John 9,
for example, when His disciples met a man blind from
birth, they asked, "How did this man get into this situation? Why did it happen? Who sinned, this man or his parents, that he was born this way?"

In answering, Jesus said in effect, "You're asking the
wrong question. This man was born blind so that the
power of God could be displayed in his life." The Savior
then anointed the man's eyes with mud, which he was to
wash away in the pool of Siloam. "So he went and washed,
and came back seeing."

Later, in John 11, we read of two sisters, Mary and
Martha, who sent Christ an urgent message regarding
their brother, Lazarus, who was dying. "Come quickly,"

they said. "He whom you love is sick." But Jesus tarried till Lazarus passed away. The sisters said reprovingly, "Lord, if You had been here, our brother would not have died." Jesus saw things differently. He explained, "This sickness is not unto death, but for the glory of God, that the Son of God may be glorified through it." Then He raised Lazarus from death to life to the glory of God.

Shortly afterward, in John 12, Jesus arrived in Jerusalem on Palm Sunday. His time was short; by the end of the week He would be hanging on the cross. As He rode His little colt into the city, a spontaneous parade developed. Ecstatic crowds cheered Him like a conquering hero, shouting, "Hosanna! Blessed is He who comes in the name of the LORD!"

But Jesus didn't share their exuberance, for He foresaw His suffering. "Now My soul is troubled, and what shall I say?" He cried. "'Father, save Me from this hour'? But for this purpose I came to this hour. Father, glorify Your name" (John 12:27–28).

In other words, at the onset of the most excruciating week of His life, Jesus asked not, "How can I get out of this?" but "How can God's name be glorified?" The Father's response is in verse 28: "I have both glorified it and will glorify it again."

God doesn't waste suffering. If He leads us into impossible spots, He will deliver us in His own time, in His own way, and for His name's sake. Our job amid the difficulty is to learn our Lord's simple but submissive prayer: *What shall I say? Save me from this hour? No, Father, glorify Your name.*

That is, after all, what our lives are about. To Him alone belongs the glory. "Not unto us, O LORD, not unto us, but to Your name give glory," said the psalmist (Ps. 115:1). The children of Israel didn't understand this, so they cried, "How did we get into this mess?" They should have been asking, "How will God gain glory through this situation?"

The writer of Psalm 106 made this very point:

Our fathers in Egypt did not understand Your wonders;
They did not remember the multitude of Your mercies,
But rebelled by the sea—the Red Sea.
Nevertheless He saved them *for His name's sake.* (vv. 7–8,
    emphasis added)

How, then, did God take an impossible situation, flip it around, and use it for His honor? The story of parted waters shows us that God gains glory

when His enemies are defeated;

when His children are delivered;

when His name is exalted;

when His exploits are remembered; and

when His praises are sounded.

"God sometimes raises difficulties in the way of His people," said Matthew Henry, "that He may have the glory of subduing them, and helping His people over them."

The Lord devises ways of turning difficulties into deliverances and problems into praise. He gives beauty for ashes and an attitude of worship for the spirit of heaviness. He *will* glorify His name in the lives of His children, whatever their afflictions. He *will* gain honor for Himself over our adversarial situations. In the process, He will leave behind such blessings as make the burdens melt away like wax in the sunshine.

In His Own Way

The sorest afflictions never appear intolerable, except when we see them in the wrong light.

—BROTHER LAWRENCE

A little gospel song, now mostly forgotten, delighted Christians of a hundred years ago. Often sung to the strains of a fiddle, it boasted of God's unique methods in meeting the needs of His children.

> In some way or other the Lord will provide.
> It might not be my way. It might not be thy way.
> And yet in His own way, the Lord will provide.

With the same confidence we can say that in some way or other God will deliver His people from every trial and trouble they encounter. It might not be *my* way. It might not be *thy* way. And yet *in His own way,* the Lord will deliver. He will do it for His own name's sake; He will do it for His glory.

In the Red Sea account, the Lord intended from the beginning to gain glory for Himself by snatching His people from the jaws of annihilation at the last moment. He never worried about the outcome, knowing He could provide an escape route at any time. "God is faithful," affirms the Bible, "who . . . will also make the way of escape" (1 Cor. 10:13).

Admittedly the Lord doesn't always deliver us from our problems in the way we want Him to. He does it *His way*, but in the long run *His way* is always best, and it always leads to worship. We hear Him speak in Psalm 50:15: "Call upon Me in the day of trouble; I will deliver you, and you shall glorify Me."

I thought of this verse some time ago when a friend called, deeply troubled for her sixteen-year-old son. He had fallen into the wrong crowd, had dropped out of school, was using drugs, and was spiraling out of control. Now Jason had been arrested for assault and armed robbery. Sobbing on the phone, she told me how she loved her boy, but her problems with him were beyond solution.

As she drove to the juvenile detention center, she needed windshield wipers for her eyes, for she could hardly see the road for the tears. But she arrived to find God at work, answering her prayers. Jason, dressed in prison fatigues, was also weeping. He wanted a Bible, and he wanted to turn his life around. Like the prodigal son, he had come to his senses, and spiritually speaking, he was ready to return home. From that day he has been a different person.

"Many prodigals don't return until the twenties or thirties," I later told her. "Yours came home at age sixteen."

Like the experience of the Israelites at the Red Sea, the worst moment of her life was really her greatest day, for the Lord is in the business of delivering His people

. . . in His own way

    . . . in His own time

        . . . for His own glory.

"Many are the afflictions of the righteous," wrote David in Psalm 34:19, "but the LORD delivers him out of them all."

So now, instead of asking, "How can I get out of this mess?" ask, "How can God be glorified in the situation I'm facing?"

RED SEA
RULE 3

Acknowledge your enemy, but keep your eyes on the Lord.

Now it was told the king of Egypt that the people had fled, and the heart of Pharaoh and his servants was turned against the people; and they said, "Why have we done this, that we have let Israel go from serving us?" So he made ready his chariot and took his people with him. Also, he took six hundred choice chariots, and all the chariots of Egypt with captains over every one of them. . . . So the Egyptians pursued them.

—EXODUS 14:5–9

Pursued

The great tyrant has not forgotten you, and he designs your capture and re-enslavement.

—CHARLES SPURGEON

M y daughter was napping in her dormitory one day when she awoke with a start. An oppressing sense of evil invaded her room, and she felt a physical force descending upon her, pressing her into her bed as though to suffocate her. Terrified, she cried, "Lord, help me!" Instantly the malevolent force vanished, leaving her weak and weeping.

The devil sometimes launches direct, frontal attacks like that. I've read or heard of a number of such incidents. But Satan is usually more conniving and insidious. In Ephesians 6:11, Paul warned against the "wiles" of the devil.

Whenever he attacks, however, whether covertly or overtly, he is closer and crueler than we realize—like the Pharaoh of the Exodus. As the tyrant gazed over his wasted domain, he saw slave ghettos deserted like ghost towns. His building projects were suspended, and the sounds of construction had ceased. There was no pounding of hammers, scraping of rocks, or shouting of foremen. The snap of the lash was hushed. Nor was a slave nearby to draw his bath, oil his body, fetch his breakfast, or bow at his feet. Pharaoh was plundered and humbled before his countrymen. His anger rose like mercury in a thermometer.

"Summon the generals!" he roared. "Wake the troops! Harness the chariots!"

Weary soldiers flew from beds and barracks, horses bolted from their stalls, and the army mobilized in record time. "The Egyptians—with all the king's horses, chariot drivers, and army—chased the Israelites. They caught up with them while they were camped by the Red Sea" (Ex. 14:9 NCV).

Have you ever felt pursued? Oppressed? Sensed the devil nipping at your heels? Ever wondered if your simultaneous troubles were orchestrated by a fiendish, invisible hand? Suspected that your depression or anger stemmed from a malevolent source? The third Red Sea Rule says: Acknowledge your enemy, but keep your eyes on the Lord.

Consider the parallels between Pharaoh and Satan. Both are unyielding enemies, coveting the power of God for themselves. Both have been plundered by the Almighty, and both are enraged beyond endurance. Both have assembled vast armies for the destruction of God's people—yet neither seems to realize how utterly defeated he already was and is.

The Bible likens Satan to five different animals. In Genesis 3, he's a serpent trying to deceive God's people; in Matthew 13, a bird trying to despoil God's harvest. In John 10, Jesus considers him a wolf attacking God's flock. He's a lion trying to devour God's children in 1 Peter 5; and in Revelation 12, he's a dragon wanting to destroy God's Son.

The blood of Jesus Christ forgives our sins and resolves our guilt. His resurrection frees us from the fear of death, and it satisfies our need for eternal significance and happiness. The presence of the Lord surrounds us, while the promises of the Bible sustain us. His grace heals our whip wounds. Jesus said, "Therefore if the Son makes you free, you shall be free indeed" (John 8:36).

But Satan doesn't surrender his prey without a fight. He comes racing after the converted soul, chariot wheels churning the dust, seeking to discourage you, to defeat you. He pursues you with the intensity of Pharaoh. He may use your old friends, a spot of persecution, or discouraging responses by your family. He may show you a hypocrite in the church or afflict you with a general slacking of zeal. He may launch a missile of temptation right at your heart or fire a volley of trials and troubles into your life.

He tries to trap you in difficulty, to entangle you in trouble, to corner you in impossible situations, to lure you into temptation. If you're in a tough situation right now, suffering pain, worry, anguish, or illness, the devil is undoubtedly behind it to a greater or lesser degree.

Acknowledge Satan's activity, but don't be intimidated by him. You can resist him in the power of God and by the blood of Jesus Christ. In fact, our Commander in chief enjoins you to such resistance. When threatened by the devil's schemes, just memorize these verses and claim them at every turn:

> The people who know their God will be strong and will resist him. (Dan. 11:32 NLT)

> Resist the devil and he will flee from you. Draw near to God and He will draw near to you. (James 4:7–8)

> Resist him, steadfast in the faith. (1 Peter 5:9)

> Use every piece of God's armor to resist the enemy in the time of evil, so that after the battle you will still be standing firm. (Eph. 6:13 NLT)

When we rebuff the enemy in the name of Jesus Christ, when we stand our ground, when we resist his wiles and claim the victory of faith, when we shake off discouragement in the name of our Lord, Satan falls from heaven faster than lightning. He is drowned in the Red Sea of the blood of Jesus Christ.

Every time we resist the slightest temptation, we honor God. Every time we overcome even the smallest problem by trusting and obeying our Lord Jesus, God is glorified in our lives. Whenever we choose character over convenience, faithfulness over ease, or honesty over deceit, we bring honor to the Lord Himself. When we serve Him with watertight obedience even in small things, God is glorified, just as at the Red Sea.

"These things," wrote the apostle Paul about the events of Exodus, "happened as examples for us" (1 Cor. 10:6 NCV).

A Dog Called Satan

The devil often overshoots his mark.

—PETER CARTWRIGHT

A British newspaper, the *Sun,* bore the headline: "Vicar Savaged by Dog Called Satan." "A vicar," reported the paper, "is recovering from being savaged by an Alsatian called Satan. Alan Elwood, 45, was bitten all over his body and his trousers and shirt were ripped to shreds in the farm-yard attack in Westport, Somerset. 'It was terrifying. I was lucky to get out of it,' Mr. Elwood told the *Sun.*"

Rev. Elwood is neither the first nor the last Christian to be attacked by "Satan." We often underestimate the extent to which the enemy seeks to disrupt our lives.

When the apostle Paul encountered people trying to hinder his ministry and dissuade his hearers, he saw the hand of Satan (Acts 13:10). When he looked out over an unsaved audience, he blamed Satan for their lostness (Acts 26:18). The apostle lamented to young Timothy that those who reject the gospel are caught in the "snare of the devil, having been taken captive by him to do his will" (2 Tim.

2:26). Likewise, when men and women confessed Christ as Savior, Paul saw it as a clear blow to Satan's empire (Col. 1:13–14).

When Paul encountered troublemakers in the church, he discerned the crafty hand of Satan (Rom. 16:17–20).

When he became sick, he believed Satan had a hand in it. He referred to his illness as "a messenger of Satan to buffet me" (2 Cor. 12:7).

When he was unable to visit the Thessalonian church, Paul wrote, "We wanted to come to you . . . but Satan hindered us" (1 Thess. 2:18).

When Paul exercised church discipline on an erring member, he was turning such a one over to Satan (1 Cor. 5:5).

When married couples in his churches had poor sexual relationships, exacerbating temptations toward immorality, Paul blamed such lapses on the devil (1 Cor. 7:5).

When the apostle came across Gentiles worshiping idols, he knew Satan was behind it (1 Cor. 10:20–21).

When he found Christians harboring bitter or unforgiving attitudes toward others, he saw the hand of Satan. He instructed the Ephesians, "Never go to bed angry—don't give the devil that sort of foothold" (Eph. 4:26–27 PHILLIPS). He told the Corinthians to forgive the man who had sinned against them, "lest Satan should take advantage of us; for we are not ignorant of his devices" (2 Cor. 2:11).

When his converts strayed, Paul attributed their behavior

to the devil (1 Tim. 4:1; 5:15). When false teachers popped up, Paul believed they had been sent by Satan (2 Cor. 11:13–15). When local church leaders made a mess of their reputation and work, he blamed the evil one (1 Tim. 3:6–7).

"Our fight is not against any physical enemy," Paul warned. "It is against organizations and powers that are spiritual. We are up against the unseen power that controls the dark world, and spiritual agents from the very head-quarters of evil" (Eph. 6:12 PHILLIPS).

The patriarch Job would have understood Paul's concern. In one terrible season, he lost his herds to barbarians, his children to a tornado, his health to a disease, his wealth to misfortune. As he sat among the ashes scraping his boils with pottery shards and bemoaning his fate, he didn't realize that his afflictions had been orchestrated by Satan in an attempt to destroy his soul. But they had been.

The same devil orchestrates similar attacks against us today.

How do we respond? We draw near to Christ and keep ourselves under the protective cloud of His grace. In Exodus 14, Pharaoh could threaten with brawn and bluster; he could stir up frightening clouds of chariot dust; he could terrify with a thousand swords. But he was powerless to actually harm the Israelites as long as they remained under the protective cloud of God's glory and grace. "Resist him [Satan], steadfast in the faith," wrote Peter (1 Peter 5:9).

Several years ago, I was walking down a sidewalk in East Nashville, making a pastoral visit. Suddenly I saw a German shepherd flying across a lawn, barking, snarling, teeth bared, mouth frothing. I was so startled that as it lunged at me, I screamed and jumped backward. But between me and my would-be attacker, there was a chain-link fence. The dog struck the fence full force. My heart was racing, but I was utterly safe because of the protective fence.

Satan can growl and bark, lunge and threaten. But when we're enclosed by the grace of our Lord Jesus Christ, he can do us no real or lasting harm.

But we always make a mistake when we acknowledge the Lord and keep our eyes on Satan. Far better to acknowledge the devil while keeping our eyes on Christ.

For all his insights and explanations about the evil one, the apostle Paul, in reality, focused on Christ. In the Pauline letters, the word *Jesus* occurs in 219 verses, the word *Lord* in 272 verses, and the word *Christ* in 389 verses. *Satan,* on the other hand, occurs in only 10 verses, and the word *devil* in only 6.

When things are going badly, when you feel trapped between sword and sea, when you're under assault, acknowledge the devil—but keep your eyes on Christ.

He will see you through. He will make a way.

RED SEA
RULE 4

Pray!

When Pharaoh drew near, the children of Israel lifted their eyes, and behold, the Egyptians marched after them. So they were very afraid, and the children of Israel cried out to the Lord.

—EXODUS 14:10

Seaside Prayers

Their fear set them a praying, and that was a good effect of it. God brings us into straits that He may bring us to our knees.

—MATTHEW HENRY

Some situations have offered me just two options—I could either panic or pray. My tendency is to panic, like the Israelites by the Red Sea or the disciples on the Sea of Galilee. I've had my share of hyperventilating, heart-racing panic attacks. But the Lord has spent years trying to show me that prayer is the means by which I can, if I choose, stay even-tempered, self-possessed, cool-headed, and strong-spirited, even in a crisis.

When we can't press forward, move sideward, or step backward, it's time to look upward and to ask God to make a way. In a time of uncertainty, the patriarch Jacob said, "Let us arise and go up to Bethel; and I will make an altar there to God, who answered me in the day of my distress and has been with me in the way which I have gone" (Gen. 35:3).

Referring to his days as a fugitive, David wrote, "In my

distress I called upon the LORD, and cried out to my God. He heard my voice from His temple" (2 Sam. 22:7). The writer of Psalm 107 declared,

> They cry out to the LORD in their trouble,
> And He brings them out of their distresses.
> He calms the storm,
> So that its waves are still. (vv. 28–29)

That's just what happened as the Israelites cried out to God at the Red Sea, except there the waves became trembling walls of water, held back by invisible dams.

I'm not talking now about our regular, daily quiet-time prayer habits, important as they are; I'm talking about crisis-time prayers. Prayers of importunity and intensity. Prayers during life-threatening or soul-shattering events. "This kind does not go out except by prayer and fasting" (Matt. 17:21). "Pray hard and long," Paul wrote in Ephesians 6:18 (*The Message*). The Israelites were in crisis in Exodus 14, and their seaside cry was

urgent,

united,

unfeigned,

but unbelieving.

The urgency of their prayer was obvious, evidenced by the verb *cried*. I had a friend in college who gave me a little booklet her father, Cameron Thompson, had written, titled *Master Secrets of Prayer*. My copy is now underlined and tattered, but I still treasure it and have these words underlined:

> There comes a time, in spite of our soft, modern ways, when we must be desperate in prayer, when we must wrestle, when we must be outspoken, shameless and importunate. Many of the prayers recorded in Scripture are "cries," and the Hebrew and Greek words are very strong. Despite opinions to the contrary, the Bible recognizes such a thing as storming heaven—"praying through." The fervent prayer of a righteous man is mighty in its working.

I remember such times in my own life—when my father suffered a heart attack, when a job possibility blew up in my face, when a friend was overdosing on cocaine, when my child got involved in the wrong crowd. There was little I could do except plead with God. Sometimes these prayers are prolonged. Twice in my life I've spent the entire night in prayer.

Other times, however, my prayers are quite short. I've recently learned a new prayer technique from the writings of missionary Amy Carmichael. She learned it from the famous Bible teacher Dr. F. B. Meyer, who once told her that as a young man he had been irritable and hot-tempered. An older gentleman advised him to look up at the moment of temptation and say, "Thy sweetness, Lord."

Amy Carmichael developed many variations of that prayer. When meeting someone she didn't like, she would silently pray, "Thy love, Lord." In a crisis, she'd whisper, "Thy help, Lord," or "Thy wisdom, Lord."

Sometimes when I'm worried, I just lift my heart to heaven and say, "Lord . . . ," followed by the name of one for whom I'm concerned.

Looking back over the years, I've never faced a crisis in which, in response to earnest prayer, whether prolonged or instant, God didn't make a way. James 5:16 tells us: "The earnest prayer of a righteous person has great power and wonderful results" (NLT). That's the great secret of those who put their hands in the hand of the One who can part the seas.

United and Unfeigned

I must talk to Father about this!

—BILLY BRAY

One evening in my study, I grew deeply troubled over a particular situation, and my anxiety increased to paralyzing levels. I walked through the offices and found our youth minister working late. Together we knelt and earnestly prayed about the situation. Later that evening I discovered that, against all odds, the tide had turned at the very moment we had been praying.

I don't know how to explain it, but somehow, had I been praying alone, I feel my solitary prayer might not have been effective enough to produce the change. But there's something about praying with another person that intensifies prayer and sends it to heaven with greater velocity.

We learn from Exodus 14:10 that "the children of Israel cried out to the LORD." There was one great united cry, rising from a host of voices, piercing the heavens like a massive signal of distress.

When Dr. Paul White was serving in a bush hospital in

East Africa, a schoolteacher named Yamusi Cikata came to him, carried on a stretcher from a nearby village. Parasites and disease had attacked his feet, swelling them to twice their normal size. He was no longer able to walk or even stand.

"The disease is very bad indeed," Dr. White told him, following an examination. "The only way to save your life will be to cut both your legs off above the knee."

The man's face fell. "But there's no place for a man in our tribe who has no feet. How can I cultivate? How can I look after my garden and my cattle?"

Pulling a worn Testament from his scant clothing, Yamusi turned to James 5:16 and said, "Read this." Dr. White, unable to read the tribal language, asked his assistant to translate it: *The very strong prayer of a man who is right with God is most effective.*

"Do you believe that?" asked the patient.

"Yes, Yamusi, I do."

"Do you believe it enough to stake my life on it?"

The doctor pondered the question. "That depends on you as well," he finally replied. "It says in the Book, 'If two of you shall agree in anything that you ask, it will be done.'" Together the two men made a covenant, the doctor kneeling by the man's bedside. The prayers were accompanied by months of hot foot baths, injections, therapy, and treatment. After seven months, a slight improvement was seen, and the two men knelt together thanking God and asking for more progress.

One morning, Dr. White found Yamusi hobbling around the ward, beaming; and before the year was out he was able to walk without pain.[5]

God doesn't always say yes to all our requests, but He listens with unusual attentiveness when two or three gather in united prayer—and He responds in His own way and time with power and wisdom.

The Israelites' prayer was not only united, but also unfeigned. They had never been more earnest. It wasn't a religious ritual. They were panicked, and their outburst of prayer was real and raw.

Listen to the way the men and women of the Bible prayed, and compare it to your prayer life:

If you would *earnestly* seek God And make your supplication to the Almighty . . . Surely now He would awake for you. (Job 8:5–6, emphasis added)

Jairus . . . begged Him *earnestly*, saying, "My little daughter lies at the point of death. Come and lay Your hands on her." (Mark 5:22–23, emphasis added)

When they came to Jesus, they begged Him *earnestly*. (Luke 7:4, emphasis added)

And being in agony, [Jesus] prayed more *earnestly*. (Luke 22:44, emphasis added)

Elijah . . . prayed *earnestly* that it would not rain; and it did not rain on the land for three years and six months. (James 5:17, emphasis added)

Continue *earnestly* in prayer, being vigilant in it with thanksgiving. (Col. 4:2, emphasis added)

The *earnest* prayer of a righteous person has great power and wonderful results. (James 5:16 NLT)

When God, in His grace and mercy, answered the cry of the Israelites alongside the sea, it wasn't because they expected Him to.

Look at the way the passage unfolds: "The children of Israel cried out to the LORD. Then they said to Moses, 'Because there were no graves in Egypt, have you taken us away to die in the wilderness?'" (Ex. 14:10–11). They prayed, but they didn't imagine that God would actually answer their prayer.

Sad to say, I understand. Once, for example, I was spending the night in a crumbling high-rise in Pôrto Alegre, Brazil. A friend and I had ascended to our room on the top floor in a tiny, creaking elevator. From our window I saw slums spreading far beneath me, and I felt uneasy. That evening I prayed, "Lord, keep us safe tonight from fire. You can see we're at the top of a dilapidated hotel. It's nothing but a firetrap. There isn't a fire station nearby, and

I can't find any fire escapes. Lord, You know this towering old building would go up in flames in a second. Only a spark, then, *poof!* And, Lord, You saw all those stacked-up cartons of Marlboros being sold in the streets, and right now this hotel is full of people falling asleep with cigarettes in their mouths . . ."

By the time I finished praying, I was a nervous wreck; I hardly slept a wink all night. The next morning, I realized that my bedtime prayer had focused on my negative feelings rather than on God's assurances and promises, and I learned an important truth: unless we plead in faith, our prayers can do more harm than good.

How much better to offer what James called *the prayer of faith* (James 5:15).

Thomas Watson, the Puritan writer, said, "Faith is to prayer what the feather is to the arrow; it feathers the arrow of prayer, and makes it fly swifter, and pierce the throne of grace."

When you face impossible odds, pray urgently, unfeignedly, unitedly. And trust the great prayer-answering God who grants mercy and imparts grace to help in time of need.

RED SEA
RULE 5

Stay calm and confident, and give God time to work.

Moses said to the people: "Do not be afraid. Stand still, and see the salvation of the Lord, which He will accomplish for you today. For the Egyptians whom you see today, you shall see again no more forever. The Lord will fight for you, and you shall hold your peace."

—Exodus 14:13–14

Waiting

I am waiting on Thee, Lord, to open the way.

—J. HUDSON TAYLOR

One night when I was worried sick about something, I found four words sitting quietly on page 1291 of my Bible. I'd read them countless times before, but as I stared at them this time, they fairly flew at me like stones from a slingshot. The four words, now well underlined in my New International Version, are *leave room for God*.

The immediate context, Romans 12:19, involves retribution. When someone harms us, advised the writer, we shouldn't try to get even, but should leave room for God's wrath. There are times when we need to let Him settle the score. But if we can leave room for God's wrath, I reasoned, can we not, when facing other challenges, leave room for His other attributes? For His power? For His grace? For His intervention? I underlined the words *leave room for God* and have leaned on them ever since.

I cannot solve every problem, cure every hurt, or avoid every fear, but I can leave room for God. I don't have the answer to every dilemma, but I can leave room for God to work. I can't do the impossible, but He is able to do "exceedingly abundantly above all" that I could ask or imagine (Eph. 3:20). The Lord delights in the impossible.

Moses told the Israelites: "Fear not; stand still (firm, confident, undismayed) and see the salvation of the Lord which He will work for you today. For the Egyptians you have seen today you shall never see again. The Lord will fight for you, and you shall hold your peace and remain at rest" (AMPLIFIED).

This is what the biblical phrase "wait on the Lord" is about: committing our Red Sea situations to Him in prayer, trusting Him, and waiting for Him to work. Doing that runs counter to our proactive and assertive selves, but many a modern migraine would be cured by a good dose of Psalm 37:7–8: "Rest in the LORD, and wait patiently for Him . . . Do not fret—it only causes harm."

If you're in a difficult place right now, perhaps you need to entrust the problem to the Lord and leave it in His hands awhile. He alone can storm the impregnable, devise the improbable, and perform the impossible. He alone can part the waters.

Don't Be Afraid

In times of great difficulty and great expectation, it is our wisdom to keep our spirits calm, quiet, and sedate; for then we are in the best frame both to do our own work and to consider the work of God.

—MATTHEW HENRY

Some years ago, I read through the Bible, Genesis to Revelation, looking for phrases such as "fear not" and "do not be afraid." I discovered 107 such occurrences in the Old Testament, and 42 in the New Testament. Anything mentioned so frequently in the Bible must be either a common condition among humans or a great priority with God. As I studied these verses (and others dealing with similar emotions), one thing became clear: God wants His children's emotions under control.

That's hard for us. The very word *emotion* is the word *motion* with an *e* in front of it (for *erratic*, I suppose). Our feelings go up and down, sometimes with the velocity of a roller coaster. One moment we're enraged, then we're consumed with love or lust or in the throes of depression or anxiety. We have strong feelings, often driven by compelling circumstances. Yet all is worsened by giving our emotions free rein.

Maturity can be described as the ability to keep one's passions under control. My two-year-old granddaughter has little control over her emotions. When she becomes happy, she's happy all over, racing through the house like a tornado, laughing, playing, screaming. Other times she's angry top to toe, screaming, crying, and stomping her feet.

From adults we expect a maturity that says, "Don't trust your emotions, and never be controlled by them. We're to walk by faith, not by feelings. Sometimes we must choose an attitude that's contrary to the way we feel."

That's the point of Exodus 14. The children of Israel had every reason for utter terror. They were cornered like rabbits by encircling wolves, and the dust in the distance rose up like demons. The Israelites were facing not reenslavement, but the impending slaughter of their families, their little ones, their aged parents. There was no human escape.

Although there were good reasons to be afraid, there were even better reasons for remaining confident. They had an Ally alongside them who had sent lightning and locusts and a fistful of other plagues upon the Egyptians, who billowed up as a pillar of cloud and fire.

That Ally was saying: "Get a grip on yourself. Reel in these runaway emotions. Bring yourself under control.

Work your way from fear to faith. Trust Me, for I'm going to take care of this. I'm going to fight for you."

Dr. Martyn Lloyd-Jones once preached a sermon on the terror of the disciples during the storm on Galilee. He ended with a sharp conclusion: "I do not care what the circumstances may be, the Christian should never be agitated, the Christian should never be beside himself, the Christian should never be at his wit's end, should never be in a condition in which he has lost . . . It implies a lack of trust and confidence in Him."

I have seldom been so reprimanded by a sermon or so thankful for it. In our distresses in life when trapped by the Red Sea, we must trust God with the impossible and leave room for Him to work, for the Lord has promised to fight for us. Search this out in Scripture, and you'll discover it's one of the truths the Lord most often repeats. Here are some examples:

Do not be terrified . . . The LORD your God, who goes before you, He will fight for you. (Deut. 1:29–31)

You must not fear them, for the LORD your God Himself fights for you. (Deut. 3:22)

Be strong and of good courage, do not fear nor be afraid of them; for the LORD your God, He is the One who goes with you. He will not leave you nor forsake you. (Deut. 31:6)

All this assembly shall know that the LORD does not
save with sword and spear; for the battle is the LORD's.
(1 Sam. 17:47)

If God is for us, who can be against us? . . . In all these
things we are more than conquerors through Him who
loved us. (Rom. 8:31, 37)

When the Communists overran China following the end
of World War II, a thousand missionaries with China
Inland Mission (CIM) were trapped behind the Bamboo
Curtain. CIM ordered a total evacuation in January 1951,
but was it too late? Communists were not averse to killing.

Arthur and Wilda Mathews applied for exit visas on
January 3. Their living conditions had deteriorated to a
bare kitchen where, in the corner, Wilda had converted a
footlocker into a prayer nook. Days passed with no action
on their requests. Meanwhile citizens were executed on the
town's athletic field every day; from her kitchen Wilda
heard the shots. The strain grew unbearable, and she was
overwhelmed by fear.

Sunday, March 21, 1951, was, as she later called it, Black
Easter. Wilda sneaked into an Easter church service, but
when she opened her mouth to sing "He Lives!" no words
came out. Returning home, she fell at the trunk, and her
trembling fingers found 2 Chronicles 20: "The battle is not

yours, but God's. . . . You will not need to fight in this battle.
Position yourselves, stand still and see the salvation of the
LORD, who is with you, O Judah and Jerusalem! Do not fear
or be dismayed" (vv. 15, 17). Wilda clamped onto those
words, and two weeks later she wrote, "The conflict has been
terrible, but peace and quiet reign now."

Over the next two years, the Mathews family repeatedly
faced dangerous situations, their baby in harm's way, their
pantry empty, their enemies surrounding them. But Arthur
and Wilda committed each situation, one after another, into
the Lord's hands. Miraculously, in God's timing, all the
CIM missionaries got out without a single one being mar-
tyred, the last being Arthur Mathews. It was perhaps the
greatest exodus since the one in Exodus 14.[6]

Many times we cannot solve problems, heal hurts, change
circumstances, or win our own battles. We must kneel in
prayer, then stand to see what He will do. We must leave room
for God, staying calm and giving Him time to work.

"Faith," wrote C. H. Mackintosh, "raises the soul above
the difficulty, straight to God Himself, and enables one to
stand still. We gain nothing by our restless and anxious
efforts. . . . It is therefore true wisdom, in all times of difficulty and perplexity, to stand still—to wait only upon God,
and He will assuredly open a way for us."

Red Sea
Rule 6

When unsure, just take the
next logical step by faith.

*The Lord said to Moses, "Why do you cry to Me?
Tell the children of Israel to go forward."*

—Exodus 14:15

Day by Day

I have found that if we go as far as we can,
God often opens up the rest of the way.

—ISOBEL KUHN

Many years ago an English vicar, a sincere and sensitive young man, grappled with prolonged, unresolved spiritual and emotional conflict in his life that, by age thirty, had damaged his health. He took a trip to Italy for rest, but while there he contracted a fever and was confined to bed. Finally able to travel again, he booked passage aboard a sailing ship. But in the middle of the Mediterranean, the winds ceased, and the ship floundered for days. The dispirited young man could take it no longer. Alone in his cabin, he wrestled mightily with God until he gained victory in his heart. Out of that experience, John Henry Newman wrote one of the most famous hymns in the English language:

> Lead, kindly Light! Amid th' encircling gloom,
> Lead Thou me on;
> The night is dark, and I am far from home,

Lead Thou me on;
Keep Thou my feet;
I do not ask to see
The distant scene;
One step enough for me.

On the despairing shores of the Red Sea, the Israelites couldn't see what was in the distance. They had no binoculars that could view Canaan or even the opposite shore. But the Lord gave them a simple plan: *tell the children of Israel to go forward.*

The nineteenth-century expositor C. H. Mackintosh believed the Red Sea did not divide throughout all at once, but opened progressively as Israel moved forward, so that they needed to trust God for each fresh step. Mackintosh wrote, "God never gives guidance for two steps at a time. I must take one step, and then I get light for the next. This keeps the heart in abiding dependence upon God."

It is axiomatic that God generally leads His children step-by-step, provides for us day by day, and cares for us moment by moment:

"The pillar of cloud led them forward *day by day*" (Neh. 9:19 TLB, emphasis added).

"Day by day the Lord also pours out his steadfast love upon me" (Ps. 42:8 TLB, emphasis added).

"Your strength shall be renewed *day by day* like morning dew" (Ps. 110:3 TLB, emphasis added).

"Give us *day by day* our daily bread" (Luke 11:3, emphasis added). [And if our daily bread, then our daily work. Our daily plans. Our daily opportunities.]

"Blessed *day by day* be the Lord, who bears our burdens; God, who is our salvation" (Ps. 68:20 NAB, emphasis added).

"The Levites and the priests praised the LORD *day by day*, singing with loud instruments unto the LORD" (2 Chron. 30:21 KJV, emphasis added).

"Therefore we do not lose heart. Even though our outward man is perishing, yet the inward man is being renewed *day by day*" (2 Cor. 4:16, emphasis added).

As a freshman in college I grew unhappy with the school I was attending, and I prayed for guidance. Afterward I felt I should enroll in Columbia Bible College, and I did. While there, I had no idea what vocation I'd be entering, but having prayed and sought the counsel of others, I decided to go to graduate school. When an opportunity opened to travel in New England one summer, preaching and speaking at churches and camps, I went. One night at a camp somewhere in Vermont, I slipped a canoe onto the lake and paddled in the moonlight, praying and seeking

God's will. That evening the Lord whispered in my ear that He wanted me in the pastorate.

After Katrina and I were married, a dozen churches interviewed us, but no one offered us a position, so I took a temporary job at Sears. By and by, a lovely little church in the country hired us, followed a few years later by a church in suburban Nashville, Tennessee, where we've been for more than twenty years.

Whenever I haven't known what to do, I've just tried to do what comes next, to take the next logical step by faith. I've decided that sometimes plodding is better than plotting when it comes to finding God's will, and I've often been encouraged by the words of this much-loved hymn:

> Day by day and with each passing moment,
> Strength I find to meet my trials here;
> Trusting in my Father's wise bestowment,
> I've no cause for worry or for fear.
> *("Day by Day" by Karolina W. Sandell-Berg)*

And in the footsteps of Jesus, neither do you.

Step by Step

How it pays to take one step at a time with God!

—Isobel Kuhn

Worn out by a spell of sleepless nights, I sat down to figure out what was bothering me. I jotted down four problems and realized I had been paralyzed by procrastination. None of my dilemmas had simple solutions, so I kept putting off dealing with them. After writing them down, I asked a simple question about each one: "What little step can I take right now toward addressing this?"

One required a phone call, and with another I had to make a tentative decision. The third problem needed a conversation, and the fourth was a matter of sitting down with my calendar. I wasn't able to tackle the whole of each problem at once, but I got off dead center by figuring out the next step regarding each issue.

My daughter and son-in-law are doing the same with their finances. Like many young couples, they started marriage with too much debt. Now they have cut up their credit cards, reduced their spending, and started paying off their bills—

starting with the smallest. Step-by-step they're gaining ground in their pursuit of financial security.

We're never sure what will happen a year from now. But the next step is often more or less obvious if we'll think about it; so in facing any vexing problem, make up your mind to prayerfully take the next logical step by faith.

Dale Carnegie began his famous book *How to Stop Worrying and Start Living*, published in the 1940s, by describing a medical student who was profoundly anxious about the future—graduating from school, establishing a practice, making a living. He was working himself into a nervous breakdown. Then one spring day in 1871 he read twenty-one words from the writings of Thomas Carlyle that changed his thinking. The young man later became the most famous physician of his era. He organized the Johns Hopkins School of Medicine and became Regius Professor of Medicine at Oxford. He was knighted by the king of England, and he became the subject of numerous biographies.

His name was Sir William Osler, and these are the words he read: "Our main business is not to see what lies dimly at a distance, but to do what lies clearly at hand."[7]

Jesus taught us in the Sermon on the Mount: "So don't be anxious about tomorrow. God will take care of your tomorrow too. Live one day at a time" (Matt. 6:34 TLB).

There's a lovely verse in Genesis 24, spoken by Abraham's

servant Eliezer while on a mission to Mesopotamia to find a bride for Isaac. Arriving there, he met Rebekah and explained to her family his mission. In Genesis 24:27 (KJV), we have this telling phrase: "I being in the way, the LORD led me."

When the Communists overran China, missionary Isobel Kuhn escaped on foot with her young son, Danny, across the dangerous snow-covered Pienma Pass. She finally arrived at Myitkyina in Upper Burma, but there she was stranded "at the world's end" without money, unable to speak the language, and still half a globe away from home. "I cannot tell you the dismay and alarm that filled me," she later wrote.

But in her perplexity, she made two decisions. "The first thing is to cast out fear," she said. "The only fear a Christian should entertain is the fear of sin. All other fears are from Satan sent to confuse and weaken us. How often the Lord reiterated to His disciples, 'Be not afraid!'" So Isobel knelt and spread her heart before Him. "I refused to be afraid and asked Him to cast such fears out of my heart."

Her second determination was to "seek light for the next step." She had no idea how to get out of Asia, but with God's help she could figure out what to do that day to provide food and funds, to find a safe place to stay, to find a means of communicating with the outside world.

Eventually she arrived back home, safe and sound, but

it came by trusting God for guidance in small increments, taking the journey one footprint at a time.[8]

When you don't know what to do next, cast out fear and seek light for the next step. Trust God for guidance in small increments; and if you can't see what lies dimly in the distance, do what lies clearly at hand.

Moment by Moment

It was a path where faith alone could walk, and step by step in faith they trod it until the other shore was reached.

—JOHN RICHIE

I recently read of a woman whose husband was murdered. When the news hit her, she nearly collapsed; but, excusing herself long enough to sit down and collect her thoughts, she offered the Lord a simple prayer: "I asked Him to help me to know what to do next and to be calm enough to do it."

In 1 Samuel 9, Saul went looking for his father's lost donkeys, never dreaming the entire trip had been orchestrated by the Lord to lead the teenager to the prophet Samuel. When at last the two met, Samuel anointed Saul king over Israel and told him something to this effect: "Now when you leave here, *this is* going to happen, and *that is* going to happen, and then *something else* is going to happen. Things will unfold for you like signs, step-by-step."

As we read in verse 7: "And let it be, when these signs come to you, that you do as the occasion demands; for God is with you."

Or as the Living Bible puts it, "From that time on your decisions should be based on whatever seems best under the circumstances, for the Lord will guide you."

It was, in essence, the same plan God employed for the Israelites by the Red Sea. At the moment of their greatest perplexity, the Red Sea divided before them, and they took their first hesitant steps into the midst of the piled-up waters, timidly testing the sea floor and finding it a highway of hope—one that had to be traveled step-by-step, moment by moment.

In the process they discovered the lesson later expressed by this beloved hymn, which is true now for you and me:

> Never a trial that He is not there,
> Never a burden that He does not bear,
> Never a sorrow that He does not share,
> Moment by moment, we're under His care.
> *("Moment by Moment" by Daniel W. Whittle)*

If a renowned painter worked twenty years on a watercolor of a luxuriant apple tree, he would unveil it all at once. But God, wanting us to be trees planted by rivers of water and bearing fruit in season, grows us a bit at a time, from seed to sprout to seedling to sapling, through rain and wind and storm. The hot days are tough, the cold nights often worse. But, being the son of an apple grower, I can tell you that cold nights are necessary for a harvest of crisp apples. We mustn't doubt in the darkness what God has showed us in the light. We mustn't collapse when faced with adversity. Following God's will isn't a matter of unveiling, but unfolding. The One who knows the faraway future reveals each close-at-hand-step as needed.

"To go as I am led, to go when I am led, to go where I am led"; A. T. Pierson once wrote, "it is that which has been for twenty years the one prayer of my life."

Take things moment by moment, and when you don't know what to do, just do what comes next. Trust God to lead you a step at a time.

RED SEA
RULE 7

Envision God's
enveloping presence.

The Angel of God, who went before the camp of Israel, moved and went behind them; and the pillar of cloud went from before them and stood behind them. So it came between the camp of the Egyptians and the camp of Israel. Thus it was a cloud and darkness to the one, and it gave light by night to the other, so that the one did not come near the other all that night.

—Exodus 14:19–20

God's Presence in the Trial

For your Van-guard is the Lord, and your Rear-guard is the God of Israel.

—Isaiah 52:12 (ROTHERHAM)

The Angel of God, who went before the camp of Israel, moved and went behind them." Who is this angel of God accompanying the Israelites in Exodus 14? The previous chapter told us, "The LORD went before them by day in a pillar of cloud . . . and by night in a pillar of fire" (Ex. 13:21). The prophet Isaiah later explained that the "Angel of His Presence" saved the Israelites (Isa. 63:9).

The pillar of fire and cloud, in theological language, was a theophany or a Christophany, a singular Old Testament appearance of God Himself, specifically of God the Son, second person of the Trinity, who manifests the Father's presence (John 1:18).

In other words, the Lord Himself ushered the Israelites through the Red Sea: "The Angel of God, who went before the camp of Israel, moved and went behind them . . . So it came between the camp of the Egyptians and the camp of

70

Israel. Thus it was a cloud and darkness to the one, and it gave light by night to the other, so that the one did not come near the other all that night" (Ex. 14:19–20).

What a perfect description of our Lord Jesus who gives light to those who trust Him; but to those who reject Him, utter darkness. He comforts the one and confounds the other. He is a Savior to the one, and a Judge to the other.

For His children, He serves as both Guard and Guide. He both precedes us and protects us. He is simultaneously our Shepherd and Shield. He is Alpha and Omega, the first and the last, the One who goes before, guiding into the future, and the One who goes behind, gathering up our debris, our failures, and our poor attempts at ministry, blessing us and leaving a blessing behind us for others.

Consider what the psalmist declared,

I look behind me and you're there,
        then up ahead and you're there, too—
        your reassuring presence, coming and going.
This is too much, too wonderful—
        I can't take it all in! (Ps. 139:5–6 *The Message*)

As the mountains surround Jerusalem,
So the LORD surrounds His people
From this time forth and forever. (Ps. 125:2)

God surrounds His people with favor "as with a shield" (Ps. 5:12). God surrounds His people with "songs of deliverance"; mercy surrounds those who trust in the Lord (Ps. 32:7, 10). We pray along with the psalmist: "Lord, let your constant love surround us, for our hopes are in you alone" (Ps. 33:22 TLB).

At the Red Sea, God put His people in a position where His presence had never been so real to them. Using difficulty, He cultivated within them a greater appreciation for Himself. "God's presence *in the trial* is much better than exemption *from the trial*," wrote one commentator. "The Lord's presence is never so sweet as in moments of appalling difficulty."

When you find yourself between sword and sea, remember that difficult times can sensitize us to God's nearness. He's never so close as when we're shipwrecked on omnipotence and driven by despair into His chambers where we find Him "a very present help in trouble" (Ps. 46:1).

Envision His enveloping presence, and learn to say, "I will fear no evil, for You *are* with me"—even in dark valleys and by hostile seas.

Four Suggestions

He is first and He is last, and we are gathered up between, as in great arms of eternal lovingkindness.

—AMY CARMICHAEL

After my father's passing, my mother struggled pitifully with loneliness. There was little anyone could do for it. Her rambling mountain house seemed desolate, haunted with memories of a vanished hand and a silenced voice. But she was a sturdy woman with an unusual streak of determination, and as time passed, she began to discover some of the benefits of living alone, such as God's presence.

She later told me, "I've adjusted nicely to the single life, for I've never been so sure I'm *not* alone. The Lord and I talk together all day. When I wake up in the morning, He's waiting to greet me, and when I go to bed at night, He stays up and stands guard."

Though she was a lifelong Christian, my mother's latter years were marked by renewed love for the Scripture, busy ministry to others, a deepened prayer life, and accelerated growth in praise and worship.

How can you master the practice of the presence of God? First, *affirm His nearness in your heart.* The psalmist was doing that when he exclaimed in Psalm 139:5–6, "You have hedged me behind and before. . . . Such knowledge is too wonderful."

Throughout the Bible we find God's people affirming this reality in their hearts. By memorizing and claiming some of the following verses, you, too, can instantly remind yourself of God's presence in any and every situation:

- The Lord is near. Do not be anxious about anything. (Phil. 4:5–6 NIV)

- Fear not, for I am with you. (Isa. 41:10)

- Behold, I am with you and will keep you wherever you go. (Gen. 28:15)

- Speak, and do not keep silent; for I am with you. (Acts 18:9–10)

- I will never leave you nor forsake you. (Heb. 13:5)

The practice of frequently reminding ourselves of the Lord's abiding presence, suggested an ancient mystic, will eventually, if attempted diligently, become habitual and soon thereafter become natural.

Second, *visualize God's presence in your mind.* Often when I pray, I look at a nearby chair and talk to God as though He were sitting there; I speak to Him naturally as to a friend. It isn't a matter of projecting an imaginary image of God and pretending He's there. It's a matter of recognizing the presence of the God who *really is* there.

One of my daughters told me she sometimes goes to sleep visualizing the Lord holding her in His arms as I held her in the rocking chair when she was small. The biblical writers used such imagery. For example, in Deuteronomy 33:27 we read, "The eternal God is your refuge, and underneath are the everlasting arms." The psalmist said, "The LORD is my shepherd; I shall not want." Jesus spoke of gathering us under His wings like a hen gathering her chicks. David visualized God as a rock of refuge to which he could continually resort. Isaiah spoke of being carried on wings like eagles. When Paul was facing the Roman tribunal, he reported, "At my first defense no one stood with me, but all forsook me. . . . But the Lord stood with me and strengthened me" (2 Tim. 4:16–17). He imagined God standing beside him in the courtroom like an omnipotent advocate and undaunted friend.

Visualizing God's presence not only bestows comfort, but it restrains sinful tendencies. The other day I was visiting a new Christian who told me he was studying his Bible, praying each day, and sharing his faith with others. But he was having one problem. Every so often, a noxious word would fly from his mouth like a sudden burp. "Well," I said, "give me an example. Go ahead and curse right now."

"Oh, no," he said with embarrassment. "I can't do that."

"Sure you can," I replied. "Let 'er fly."

"No!"

When I asked why, he replied, "You're my pastor. I can't cuss in front of you."

"Well," I said, "if you're ashamed to cuss in my presence, why aren't you ashamed to do it in the Lord's presence? He's always with you."

The young man got my point. The reality of God's presence both comforts our hearts and restrains our behavior.

Third, *access God's nearness through prayer.* During my devotional time recently I came across James 4:8: "Draw near to God."

"How?" I wondered. The cross-reference took me to Deuteronomy 4:7 where I found the answer: "What other nation is so great as to have their gods near them the way the LORD our God is near us *whenever we pray to him?*" (NIV, emphasis added).

The best way to develop an abiding awareness of God's presence is to speak to Him often in prayer. Prayer is the environment in which we most solidly connect with God on an intimate basis. We may not always *feel* His presence in an emotional sense, but *by faith* we enter His presence in a vital spiritual sense.

When Dwight Moody was asked how he managed to remain so intimate in his relationship with Christ, he replied, "There isn't any problem in my life, there isn't any uncertainty in my work but I turn and speak to Him as naturally as to someone in the same room, and I have done it these years because I can trust Jesus."

Fourth, *reflect His presence in your demeanor.* Nicholas Herman (pronounced är-män´) was born in Lorraine, France, in 1605. He reached his teen years at the onset of the Thirty Years' War, during which he fought for the French army, was seriously wounded, and walked with great difficulty for the rest of his life. Converted at age eighteen, he became an assistant for a local official in the French Treasury.

Years passed, and at age fifty, wanting a richer spiritual life, Nicholas joined a Carmelite monastery in Paris. But he was assigned to the kitchen, a task that struck him as insulting and humbling. For several years, he went about his chores grudgingly but dutifully.

One day Nicholas decided to change his thinking. He began frequently reminding himself of how constantly God's presence hovered about him. Even the most menial tasks, Nicholas realized, if undertaken for God's glory, are holy; and wherever the Christian stands—even in a hot, thankless kitchen—is holy ground, for the Lord is there too.

Nicholas's countenance and demeanor gradually

changed, and others began asking him a reason for his radiance. Christian leaders sought him out and valued his advice. One man, the abbot of Beaufort, was particularly impressed. The two met four times and exchanged fifteen letters to discuss Nicholas's walk with the Lord. The abbot made notes of the conversations and preserved the letters, compiling them into *The Practice of the Presence of God*. It was published in the mid-1600s, attributed to "Brother Lawrence," the name by which Nicholas was known in the monastery.

The pillar of fire and cloud followed the Israelites through the wilderness, then disappeared when they entered the promised land. But not really. It was later seen in the spectacular clouds of glory that filled Solomon's temple, and again in the ball of fire that burst into the Upper Room on the day of pentecost. The same presence now resides in and around all Christians, everywhere, at every moment. You are not facing your difficulty alone, for the Lord is closer than a friend or brother. Envision His enveloping presence right now.

RED SEA
RULE 8

Trust God to deliver in His own unique way.

Moses stretched out his hand over the sea; and the Lord caused the sea to go back by a strong east wind all that night, and made the sea into dry land, and the waters were divided. So the children of Israel went into the midst of the sea on the dry ground, and the waters were a wall to them on their right hand and on their left.

—EXODUS 14:21–22

His Miraculous Ways

There came a mighty wind like a wedge and split that sea wide open, clear to its center.

—B. H. CARROLL

The Israelites, stock-still and silent, watched in unbearable suspense as the old man raised his rod over the obstructing sea. An eastern wind suddenly gusted from heaven, tugging at the beards and cloaks of the multitude, who were mostly skeptics. They watched slack jawed as the downdraft intensified, hit the water, and slowly plowed through the sea. The waves rose in foam and fury, forming translucent walls that became an avenue for them and, later, an ambush for their enemies. A gateway to the one and a graveyard to the other.

It was the Old Testament's most dramatic object lesson, one of God's greatest miracles. Its simple lesson: trust God to deliver in His own unique way. That's His specialty.

The LORD your God walks in the midst of your camp, to deliver you. (Deut. 23:14)

Many are the afflictions of the righteous,
But the LORD delivers him out of them all. (Ps. 34:19)

He shall deliver you in six troubles,
Yes, in seven no evil shall touch you. (Job 5:19)

The Lord knows how to deliver the godly out of
temptations. (2 Peter 2:9)

[Christ] gave Himself for our sins, that He might
deliver us from this present evil age. (Gal. 1:4)

Call upon Me in the day of trouble;
I will deliver you, and you shall glorify Me. (Ps. 50:15)

The Lord will deliver me from every evil work and
preserve me for His heavenly kingdom. To Him be
glory forever. (2 Tim. 4:18)

But does He still? Does He deliver from financial woes?
Marital problems? Emotional confusion? Harm and dan-
ger? Self-destructive habits? Disease?

Yes, absolutely. But we must have God's perspective on
deliverance, for He doesn't always view things as we do.
"My thoughts are not your thoughts," the Lord cautions
in Isaiah 55:8, "nor are your ways My ways." We must

view God's deliverance not by emotional reflex, human standards, or even common sense—but by biblical truth.

God will deliver His children from every evil work, from every peril and problem, from tribulation, even from death itself. But there are no cookie cutters in heaven. God doesn't have standardized, same-size-fits-all solutions to our various problems. He treats every situation as singular and special, and He designs a unique, tailor-made deliverance to every trial and trouble.

Does He still cleave the seas? Do miracles still occur? Real miracles?

Yes, when He chooses. Here are some examples.

Christin Claypool from Kirby Free Will Baptist in Detroit took a missions trip to Cuba. Wanting to smuggle Spanish Bibles to a community of Christians there, Christin wore several layers of clothing to conserve space in her suitcase for the contraband. But her odd appearance drew the attention of security agents at every airport. Christin had to open her suitcase at her departure city, then again in the Bahamas.

Arriving in Cuba, she was alarmed to again be singled out and ordered to open her suitcase. The zipper wouldn't budge, and she could open it only about two inches. She fought with it until at length the guard impatiently took over the struggle. Despite prolonged effort, the zipper wouldn't budge. Christin was perplexed, for it was a new suitcase and had been opened several times before. In exasperation, the guard finally shoved it toward her and told her to go on.

Arriving at her hotel, Christin looked for a knife to cut open her luggage, but when she gave the zipper a tug, it opened easily. The Bibles were distributed as intended.

Another modern-day miracle occurred early in the history of the Pacific Garden Mission of Chicago, which got its start in the 1880s, when a notorious saloon called the Pacific Beer Garden was leased by a sweet Christian couple, George and Sarah Clarke. Dropping the word *Beer,* they added the word *Mission* and launched a ministry to downtrodden men and women.

In the early years, Colonel and Mrs. Clarke bore the cost of the work themselves, but the ministry's growth depleted their funds. Eventually they couldn't pay the rent, and Colonel Clarke had only twenty-four hours to make payment; otherwise they would lose their lease.

Colonel and Mrs. Clarke prayed throughout the night, reminding the Lord of the luckless whose lives were being salvaged. Emerging from their house at daybreak, they gasped. Their yard was blanketed in white. Looking closer, they discovered the lawn was covered with rare mushrooms of highest quality, though it wasn't the season for mushrooms.

Gathering the crop, the Clarkes carted the mushrooms down to the Palmer House and sold them to the chefs for enough money to pay the rent. Years later, "Mother" Clarke, commenting on the experience, said, "No mushrooms were ever seen there before—nor any since."[9]

In her biography *Go Home and Tell,* Bertha Smith tells of traveling by rickshaw to a primitive village in China to devote several days to evangelistic work. Her living conditions were squalid; she shared a stall with an ox and with swarms of flies.

Finally she prayed, "Lord, I am one of Your spoiled children. All my life I have been accustomed to screened houses and clean food. Now, I just can't eat with those flies all over my food. Down in Egypt You had flies come and go at Your word. You are the same today. . . . Now please do one of two things for me: either take the flies away, or enable me just to go ahead and eat and not mind them. You then take care of any disease germs which they may put into my body. . . . Whichever You wish to do will be good enough for me!"

Which do you think God did?

"Not a fly flew into that ox stall the remaining five days that I was there witnessing and teaching!" wrote Bertha. "You will agree that was a miracle."[10]

God can jam zippers, grow mushrooms, evict flies, and carve pathways through the sea whenever He wishes. His arm is not too short to save, nor His ear too dull to hear. Cameron Thompson said, "We have a God who begins with the impossible and goes on from there." So remember . . .

When the children of Israel were trapped and afraid
'twix forbidding tides and Pharaoh's tirade,
Jehovah commanded, and Moses obeyed.
As pitiful prayers filled an impossible place,
as Moses gazed into Jehovah's dread face,
as the people of God needed infinite grace,
the mighty winds howled; violent waves dashed.
The seawaters quivered and the lightnings flashed.
The thunders boomed and the breakers crashed.
And when the sun arose on that terrible day
the children of Israel, through the misty spray,
discovered their God had made them a way.
And many a Christian in the years that have passed
Though troubled by fears, though tired and harassed,
Have found the same God strong, sure, and steadfast.
(Robert J. Morgan)

His Providential Ways

When the light of divine providence has once shone upon a godly man, he is then relieved and set free not only from the extreme anxiety and fear that were pressing him before, but from every care.

—JOHN CALVIN

Though miracles still occur, God uses them sparingly. Even in Scripture, miracles were not God's standard operating procedure. Many people assume the Bible is packed with miracles, but it isn't. Only during certain periods in biblical history were there clusterings of signs and wonders—during the Exodus, during the ministries of Elijah and Elisha, during the life of Christ and the early days of the apostles.

Throughout most of the Bible, God helped His people in ordinary, providential ways rather than in overtly supernatural ones. The same is true today. That's why mature Christians pay special attention to the accidents, misfortunes, and coincidences that befall them. For in reality, there are no such things. Only the providential ordering of a God who watches over His prayerful, trusting children, and whose unseen hand is guiding, guarding, arranging, and rearranging circumstances.

Last year our youth minister, Mike Hollifield, and I were traveling to Sweden to teach at Holsby Brunn Bible School. As we left Nashville, the airline agent looked at our tickets with concern. "There's a mistake here," she said. "I'll correct it or you may have trouble getting back." After a few minutes at the computer, she handed us new tickets, smiled, and wished us a good trip.

But when we tried to return home two weeks later, we were told that she had inadvertently canceled our westbound flights. Our names were nowhere in the computers, and our tickets were worthless. After hours of negotiation and anxious waiting, we were finally squeezed onto an oversold flight and given the least desirable seats ever assigned by an airline. But as it happened, Mike was beside a Danish businessman who was open to hearing the gospel. For six long, transatlantic hours, Mike quietly talked with him about his life and about the wonderful difference Jesus Christ could make.

It wasn't an example of airline incompetence; it was an instance of divine providence.

A few years ago, our daughter called from Columbia International University, telling us she wanted to transfer to the University of Tennessee, but she didn't want to live in the dorms. She wondered whether we would drive to Knoxville and find her an apartment near campus.

Though Katrina and I had mixed feelings about her transferring, we accepted our assignment stoically; but arriving in Knoxville, we had no idea where to look. As we drove through the streets around campus, our hearts sank. Scores of buildings had ROOMS TO RENT signs, but they were rough and rundown. I didn't want Hannah in any of them, and we made no inquiries.

Pulling to the curb, we bowed our heads in prayer. I had recently been studying the book of Genesis, so I prayed, "Lord, when Abraham's servant was on a mission in Genesis 24, he requested an angel to guide him. Now, please send that same angel—or one just like him—to guide us to a safe, desirable apartment for our daughter."

We pulled back into the street, turned the corner, and immediately saw a stately brick building, clean and well tended. The plaque on the side listed it as a historical site. An arched entrance opened into a grassy square with a bubbling fountain. "That looks like an apartment building," I told Katrina. "I think I'll check."

"Don't waste your time," she replied. "We could never afford it."

I checked anyway. As I walked through the courtyard, I came upon an older woman, purse and keys in hand, who eyed me warily. She was the manager, and she said the apartments were primarily for graduate students and career professionals. "We like it very quiet here. No parties. We turn undergrads away."

But as we talked, she began to warm up. She finally admitted to having one small efficiency available, and, yes she would rent it to us for Hannah—"if I like her when I meet her." When she told me the price, I stifled a smile. It was less than the flophouses around the corner. Today Hannah is still safely quartered in that apartment. I'm certain the Lord sent an angel to guide us.

In the unfolding of His providence, burdens become blessings, tears lead to triumph, and the redemptive grace of God overcomes the undercurrents of life in the experiences of His children. For them, all things work together for good to those who love the Lord and are called according to His purposes.

No wonder Charles Spurgeon once quipped, "We believe in the providence of God, but we do not believe half enough in it."

His Mysterious Ways

God marks across some of our days, "Will explain later."

—Vance Havner

And then there are God's mysterious deliverances. In the "faith chapter" of the Bible (Hebrews 11), after citing some miraculous and providential escapes for God's people, the writer suddenly changes tone:

> Others were tortured, not accepting deliverance, that they might obtain a better resurrection. Still others had trial of mockings and scourgings, yes, and of chains and imprisonment. They were stoned, they were sawn in two, were tempted, were slain with the sword. They wandered about in sheepskins and goatskins, being destitute, afflicted, tormented—of whom the world was not worthy. (vv. 35–38)

When God does not deliver overtly (through a miracle) or covertly (by providence), He will deliver mysteriously, with a deeper level of intervention than we can discern; in the end it will be better for us, though for a time we may be perplexed.

In his last letter, the apostle Paul boasted, "The Lord will deliver me from every evil work and preserve me for His heavenly kingdom" (2 Tim. 4:18). Yet he was beheaded days later, his body cast aside, and his head tossed into the grave after him. Was he, after all, delivered?

Yes. He was snatched away from the evil that surrounded him, removed from tears, pain, stress, and sickness, taken where Satan could no longer harass, and be present with the Lord, "which is far better."

When Vance Havner, the wry North Carolina evangelist, lost his wife to disease, he was disconsolate. But out of the experience he later wrote:

> When before the throne we stand in Him complete, all the riddles that puzzle us here will fall into place and we shall know in fulfillment what we now believe in faith— that all things work together for good in His eternal purpose. No longer will we cry "My God, why?" Instead, "alas" will become "Alleluia," all question marks will be straightened into exclamation points, sorrow will change to singing, and pain will be lost in praise.[11]

In the vortex of God's mysterious ways, John 13:7 becomes a key verse for Christians: "Jesus answered and said to him, 'What I am doing you do not understand now, but you will know after this.'"

During the Korean War, a humble Christian servant was torn from his family by the Communists, never to see them again. Pastor Im suffered years of imprisonment, locked in a dark cell and fed only a bowl of slop each day. But he kept his courage by reciting Bible verses, especially John 13:7: "What I am doing you do not understand now, but you will know after this."

This verse also carried a professor of mine through a dark period of his life. After his beloved wife, Anne, succumbed to cancer, Dr. Anthony Fortosis wrote, "Why did the Lord send this most grievous of trials? Why did He take Home a wife and mother so early in her ministry? Why? I am content that His will is always good and acceptable. 'What I do thou knowest not now, but thou shalt know hereafter' (John 13:7) is good enough for me."

William Cowper, the English poet who wrote the hymn "God Moves in a Mysterious Way," struggled all his life with melancholy. According to Ernest Emurian's *Living Stories of Famous Hymns,* Cowper wrote this hymn following a period of near suicidal depression. Calling for a carriage, Cowper ordered the driver to take him to the Ouse River, three miles away, where he planned to kill himself. The driver, sensing the state of his passenger, breathed a prayer of thanks when dense fog enveloped the area, and he purposely lost his way in the fog, jogging up one road and down another as Cowper fell into a deep sleep. Several hours passed, the driver going in circles, letting his passenger rest. Finally he returned Cowper to his home.

"We're back home?" exclaimed Cowper. "How is that?"

"Got lost in the fog, sir. Sorry." Cowper paid his fare, went inside, and pondered how he had been spared from self-destruction by the mercy of God. That same evening in 1774, Cowper, age forty-three, wrote this autobiographical hymn:

God moves in a mysterious way His wonders to perform;
He plants His footsteps in the sea, and rides upon the
    storm.

You fearful saints, fresh courage take; the clouds you so
    much dread
Are big with mercy and shall break in blessings on your
    head.

Judge not the Lord by feeble sense, but trust Him for His
    grace;
Behind a frowning providence He hides a smiling face.

Blind unbelief is sure to err and scan His work in vain:
God is His own interpreter, and He will make it plain.

You can well trust Him to save and deliver you from every evil work and preserve you for His heavenly kingdom. He will save and deliver in His own unique way, whether miraculous, providential, or mysterious. He always does that for His children. That's His specialty.

RED SEA
RULE 9

View your current crisis as a faith builder for the future.

The LORD saved Israel that day out of the hand of the Egyptians, and Israel saw the Egyptians dead on the seashore. Thus Israel saw the great work which the LORD had done in Egypt; so the people feared the LORD, and believed the LORD and His servant Moses.

—EXODUS 14:30–31

Treadmills for the Soul

I know He tries me only to increase my faith.

—J. HUDSON TAYLOR

We don't always know why God allows problems, but we know He intends to use them to heighten our maturity and deepen our faith. Trials and troubles are dumbbells and treadmills for the soul. They develop strength and stamina. Exodus 14 concludes by noting how the Israelites benefited from their narrow escape. It beefed up their faith for the great challenges ahead of them. The Israelites "feared the LORD, and believed the LORD and His servant Moses."

Faith has a cumulative quality to it. We amass and garner it. We grow it and lay it in store for future times. Our faith grows stronger through the seasons of life.

What exactly is faith? Not long ago in Fort Worth, a gunman walked into Wedgewood Baptist Church during a youth rally. Among those killed was fourteen-year-old Cassie Griffin. I later read in a brief account of her life that she collected frog figurines, frog trinkets, frog jewelry. According to her parents, the word *FROG* summarized her philosophy—Fully Rely On God.

That's an apt definition of faith.

I've found several others in the Bible. In Luke 1, when the Virgin Mary visited her relative Elizabeth, the latter cried out: "Blessed is she who has believed that what the Lord has said to her will be accomplished!" (v. 45 NIV). What a great definition! Faith is believing that what the Lord has said to us will be accomplished.

In Romans 4, the apostle Paul wrote that Abraham "was strengthened in his faith and gave glory to God, being fully persuaded that God had power to do what he had promised" (vv. 20–21 NIV). That's a similar definition: being fully persuaded that God has the power to do what He has promised.

In the violent storm in Acts 27, the apostle Paul shouted over the tempest: "Last night an angel of the God whose I am and whom I serve stood beside me and said, 'Do not be afraid, Paul. You must stand trial before Caesar; and God has graciously given you the lives of all who sail with you.' So keep up your courage, men, for I have faith in God that it will happen just as he told me" (vv. 23–25 NIV). There we have another definition of biblical faith: believing that things will happen just as He has told us.

Look at yet another way of putting it: "By faith Abraham, even though he was past age—and Sarah herself was barren—was enabled to become a father because he considered him faithful who had made the promise" (Heb. 11:11 NIV).

Putting all this together, we find that faith is . . .

believing that what the Lord has said to us will be accomplished.

being fully persuaded that God has the power to do what He has promised.

believing that things will happen just as He has told us.

considering Him faithful who has given us promises.

We can say therefore that *faith is making reasonable assumptions.* When we take our morning shower, we assume there's going to be water, preferably hot. When we eat our cereal, we expect it to be healthy and wholesome. Driving to work, we proceed through green lights, assuming they are red for intersecting traffic.

Every single day we live by faith in a hundred ways. Even the sincerest atheist lives by faith, not only in his atheistic philosophy, but in the very processes and procedures of everyday life. God created this universe so that the faith principle is always at work.

For Christians, faith is making reasonable assumptions about God's care and control over our lives, based on His scriptural promises. We may not understand every circumstance or appreciate every event. Sometimes we're backed up to the Red Sea with the Egyptians in pursuit. But God has given us promises, and we disappoint Him when we question His ability to keep His Word: "Then He arose and rebuked the wind, and said to the sea, 'Peace, be still!' And the wind ceased and there was a great calm. But He said to them, 'Why are you so fearful? How is it that you have no faith?'" (Mark 4:39–40).

Why indeed? As Warren Wiersbe put it, "A faith that can't be tested can't be trusted."

Faith, after all, is quantifiable. One person's faith is turbocharged while another's sputters on one cylinder. As Jesus wandered through Palestine, He had a sort of X-ray vision that penetrated hearts and measured faith. He seemed intensely interested in the quantity of faith being exercised by those who crossed His path. He said to various people,

Assuredly, I say to you, I have not found such great faith, not even in Israel! (Matt. 8:10)

O woman, great is your faith! Let it be to you as you desire. (Matt. 15:28)

Why are you fearful, O you of little faith? (Matt. 8:26)

There are degrees of faith, and Jesus richly rewards those who fully trust Him: "When Jesus saw their faith, He said to the paralytic, 'Son, be of good cheer; your sins are forgiven you'" (Matt. 9:2); and "Without faith it is impossible to please God, because anyone who comes to him must believe that he exists and that he rewards those who earnestly seek him" (Heb. 11:6 NIV).

Years ago I heard Houston pastor John Bisango speak. He described a time when his daughter Melodye Jan, age five, asked for a dollhouse. John nodded and promised to build her one, then returned to his book. But glancing out the window, he saw Melodye, arms crammed with dishes and dolls, making trip after trip until she had a great pile in the yard. He asked his wife what she was doing.

"Oh, you promised to build her a dollhouse, and she believes you. She's just getting ready for it."

"I tossed aside that book, raced to the lumberyard for supplies, and quickly built that little girl a dollhouse," John said. Why? It was her simple, childlike faith in his promise.

Brother Lawrence said, "The trust we put in God honors Him much and draws down great graces. . . . When [God] finds a soul penetrated with a living faith, He pours into it His graces and favors plentifully; there they flow like a torrent."

Are you stranded at the Red Sea just now?

Trust Him.

The Lord loves to respond to faith.

Faith Building

---

*This was done, and recorded, in order to encourage God's
people in all ages to trust Him in the greatest straits.*

—MATTHEW HENRY

Lord, increase our faith.
Lord, I believe; help Thou mine unbelief.

I've often uttered these prayers, knowing that faith isn't
something I can muster up at will; it must be given by God
and developed according to the processes He has ordained.

He is, after all, a God who grows things. Physically, each
of us began life as a tiny speck. It's a marvelous cell, for all
the characteristics of each person—sex, eye color, shoe size,
intelligence, and so forth—are determined at fertilization
by the baby's genetic code that resides in the forty-six
human chromosomes in that one cell. We begin micro-
scopically, then grow.

Faith is also a growing entity. God intends to develop us
spiritually. How? Like any good teacher, He bestows truth,
then devises tests to review and reinforce that truth, to transfer and translate it into lasting, life-changing experiences.

Like any good coach, He sits down with His players, using a game book of Scripture, gives us information, explains the rules, reviews the plays. Then comes the scrimmage. Then videotapes, chewing out, more data, and another scrimmage. It's a virtually endless cycle, but in the process good players become skilled professionals. Good people become growing disciples, and little faith grows into great faith.

That was how He worked with the children of Israel and with the disciples. With the Israelites, He gave instructions through Moses, then brought them to the edge of the Red Sea or, later, into a desert with no water. He said, "Now here's a test. Let's see if you can apply My promises to your problem."

Jesus taught the disciples on the mountainside, then loaded them into a boat and sent them into a terrific storm designed to help them apply truth to life.

The same is true for us. At church we hear the Word of God, and in our devotions we feed on the Scriptures. The Lord then sends a trial into our lives to give us an opportunity to put His teachings into practice. As we trust Him and pass the test, we're strengthened for the future.

This, then, is the principle: our faith grows when we choose to apply God's promises to today's problems and use the experiences to mature us for tomorrow's challenges. In a sense, we are storing up faith for times ahead.

That's why the Bible is so full of promises. We never

encounter any situation for which God has not provided a precious promise to bear us through it.

The Puritan Thomas Watson put it quaintly in a sermon to his little congregation in England on Sunday, August 17, 1662: "Faith lives in a promise, as the fish lives in the water. The promises are both comforting and quickening, the very breast of the gospel; as the child by sucking the breasts gets strength, so faith by sucking the breast of a promise gets strength and revives. The promises of God are bladders [flotation devices] to keep us from sinking when we come to the waters of affliction. O! trade much in the promises, there is no condition that you can be in, but you have a promise."

I have a friend right now whose life is in crisis because of her husband's relapse into cocaine abuse. She is handling it with poise and wisdom, largely thanks to a verse the Lord gave her at the onset of the trial—2 Chronicles 20:15: "Do not be afraid nor dismayed . . . for the battle is not yours, but God's." When she awakens at night in apprehension, this verse comes to mind. When the phone rings at work, she tenses only a moment before consciously reminding herself that God is fighting this battle. She's not on the other side of the Red Sea yet, but I think the waters are starting to part.

J. I. Packer stated, "In the days when the Bible was universally acknowledged in the churches as 'God's Word written,' it was clearly understood that the promises recorded in

Scripture were the proper, God-given basis for all our life of faith, and that the way to strengthen one's faith was to focus it upon particular promises that spoke to one's condition."[12]

Faith, then, is simply finding and claiming the promises of God in every situation, and, based on those promises, making logical assumptions, being fully persuaded that God has the power to do what He has promised.

> Faith, mighty faith, the promise sees
> And looks to that alone;
> Laughs at life's impossibilities
> And cries, "It shall be done!"

RED SEA
RULE 10

Don't forget to praise Him.

Moses and the children of Israel sang this song to the Lord, and spoke, saying:

> *"I will sing to the LORD,*
> *For He has triumphed gloriously!*
> *The horse and its rider*
> *He has thrown into the sea!*
> *The LORD is my strength and song,*
> *And He has become my salvation;*
> *He is my God, and I will praise Him;*
> *My father's God, and I will exalt Him."*

—Exodus 15:1–2

105

The Perspective of Praise

Wash your face every morning in a bath of praise.

—CHARLES SPURGEON

At first there was dead silence.

Picture it: a mute multitude gazing in stunned disbelief at a body of water whose powerful surges had first saved by saving, then had saved by destroying. Now the terror was over; the enemy was gone; the night was past. Nothing was left but the stillness of a shocked people at daybreak.

Finally someone breathed.

Then came a whisper, a buzzing, the rumblings of a volcano of emotion about to erupt into sky-shattering doxologies. Someone shouted, "I will sing to the LORD, for He has triumphed gloriously! The horse and its rider He has thrown into the sea!"

Another rang out: "The LORD is my strength and song, and He has become my salvation."

And another sang: "He is my God, and I will praise Him; My father's God, and I will exalt Him." The floodgates of emotion broke, and the singing burst forth. It's the first recorded song in Scripture, this glorious celebration in Exodus 15. A nation of liberated slaves sang and danced and clapped and played their timbrels to frenzied exhaustion, the roar of countless voices echoing across the desert and through the skies all the way to heaven.

"I will sing to the LORD, for He has triumphed gloriously! The horse and its rider He has thrown into the sea!"

Last Sunday I stood at the back of our church and watched us singing a medley of traditional hymns and contemporary songs. Many people were singing with heartfelt gratitude, but I was bothered by the number not joining in. Some were looking from side to side; others were shifting their feet; some were whispering to friends. A contingent of latecomers were searching for seats.

Maybe we need a crisis.

One of the reasons God puts us in tough situations—or allows us to be there—is to give us the opportunity to sound forth His praises. He expects our gratitude for His deliverances.

I have a friend who unfailingly sends his grandchildren birthday cards containing money. And each year, every one of his grandchildren sends back a "thank you" note—except one. She's a dear girl, but somehow she never gets around to thanking him for his gift. He told me it leaves him a little sad and disappointed, and he is less eager to do things for her in the future. She reminds me of the men Jesus healed of their leprosy. There were ten of them, but only one came back to express thanks.

In the seventeenth century, John Trapp wrote, "He lets out His mercies to us for the rent of our praise, and is content that we may have the benefit of them so He may have the glory."

In the history of the Christian church, some of our greatest hymns have come in the darkest moments. Take, for example, the German hymn "Now Thank We All Our God," written by Martin Rinkart (1586–1649), a Lutheran pastor in the village of Eilenberg, Saxony, son of a poor coppersmith. He began his ministry during the horrors of the Thirty Years' War as floods of refugees were streaming into the walled city of Eilenberg. Plague and famine decimated the population, and people began dying in increasing numbers. Rinkart was officiating as many as fifty funerals a day. When the Swedes demanded a huge ransom, Martin Rinkart left the safety of the walls to negotiate with the enemy, and he did it with such courage and faith that there was soon a conclusion of hostilities and the period of suffering ended.

It was out of that experience that Rinkart wrote our great hymn:

> Now thank we all our God,
> with heart and hands and voices,

who wondrous things hath done,
in whom this world rejoices;
who from our mothers' arms
hath blessed us on our way
with countless gifts of love,
and still is ours today.

How can we better "thank we all our God"? Live more praise-oriented lives? I've been working on that, and I'd like to suggest that praise and worship are the sand and cement that hold the bricks in place along life's daily pathway. Every segment of our day should be encased in praise.

Get up early tomorrow morning and drink your coffee or juice on the back porch, deck, or balcony. Listen to nature's tenured professors of praise, the birds. Hear them raise their Hallelujah Chorus. Notice the beauty of sky and grass, and sing a verse of "How Great Thou Art." Learn to praise God for blessings both large and small. The other day while mowing, I saw a blanket of tiny blue flowers poking up beneath the grass. I stopped my mower, got down on my knees, and studied one. It was a miniature masterpiece, and I just took a moment to thank God for His creative genius.

I've pulled out some old tapes of Christian music I haven't used in years and started listening to them again in my car's cassette payer. I've turned off talk radio, and I've even been listening less to Christian stations, making my car a personal sound studio where I can sing to my heart's content: "O worship the King, all glorious above . . ."

During your daily prayer times, instead of rattling off all your problems to the Lord like a grocery list, spend a few minutes thanking Him for things you've never thought of mentioning before. Learn to accentuate the positive, and remember that the silver lining *is* the reality.

Be faithful in attending church, and while you're there, concentrate on the worship you're rendering and on the God you're praising.

Develop the perspective of praise.

While studying Revelation 18–19 this week, I've been impressed with the power of a proper perspective. Revelation 18 describes the destruction of the future city of Babylon, worldwide headquarters of the evil empire of the Antichrist. In one hour, the greatest city in the world will become a smoldering heap of ruins, and those watching from afar will weep and mourn, throwing dust on their heads, crying out, wailing, and saying, "Alas, alas, that great city . . . ! For in one hour your judgment has come" (v. 10).

But in chapter 19, the scene shifts to heaven where the angels and elders, witnessing the same event, are exuberant: "I heard a loud voice of a great multitude in heaven, saying, 'Alleluia! . . . Alleluia! Her smoke rises up forever

and ever! . . . Amen! Alleluia! . . . Praise our God, all you
His servants and those who fear Him, both small and
great! . . . Alleluia! For the Lord God Omnipotent reigns!'"
(vv. 1, 3–6).

Whether we have an "Alas!" or an "Alleluia!" depends on
our perspective.

Not long ago, I awoke early in a hotel in another city and
turned on the weather report. I was returning home from a
speaking engagement, and the forecast was troubling.
Violent storms. Strong winds. Lightning. Arriving at the
airport, I glanced at the menacing sky with foreboding. The
clouds were iron gray and angry.

We took off with a sharp ascent, and the plane pierced
the clouds and leveled off at a high altitude above them.
The scene was breathtaking. Bright and majestic and
peaceful and glorious—mountains of sunlit clouds rising
and falling below me as far as eye could see. They were the
same clouds, but my perspective was different. Storms, I
realized, look different from the upper side.

Colossians 3:1–3 tells us, "If then you were raised with
Christ, seek those things which are above, where Christ is,
sitting at the right hand of God. Set your mind on things
above, not on things on the earth. For you died, and your
life is hidden with Christ in God."

If wisdom, as someone said, is seeing things from
God's point of view, praise is the natural reaction to that

viewpoint. It's our typical expression of joyful confidence and triumphant thanksgiving at what God has done, is doing, and is going to do.

So whether you are on the upper side or the underside of the storm, whether you are on the east bank or the west bank of the Red Sea, God will make a way.

And as He does, don't forget to praise Him.

THE RED SEA
RULES

RULE 1
Realize that God means for
you to be where you are.

RULE 2
Be more concerned
for God's glory than
for your relief.

RULE 3
Acknowledge your
enemy, but keep your
eyes on the Lord.

RULE 4
Pray!

RULE 5
Stay calm and confident,
and give God time to work.

RULE 6
When unsure, just take the
next logical step by faith.

RULE 7
Envision God's
enveloping presence.

RULE 8
Trust God to deliver
in His own unique way.

RULE 9
View your current
crisis as a faith builder for
the future.

RULE 10
Don't forget to
praise Him.

Notes

1. This is a true story, but the name and location have been changed for security reasons.

2. Darlene Deibler Rose, *Evidence Not Seen: One Woman's Faith in a Japanese P.O.W. Camp* (Carlisle, UK: OM Publishing, 1988).

3. V. Raymond Edman, *The Disciplines of Life* (Minneapolis: World Wide Publications), 54.

4. A. W. Tozer, *We Travel an Appointed Way* (Camp Hill, PA: Christian Publications, 1988), 3.

5. Paul White, *Doctor of Tanganyika* (Grand Rapids: Eerdmans, 1941), 66–69.

6. Isobel Kuhn, *Green Leaf in Drought* (Singapore: Overseas Missionary Fellowship [IHQ] Ltd., 1997), chapter 7.

7. Dale Carnegie, *How to Stop Worrying and Start Living* (New York: Simon and Schuster, 1948), 1.

8. Isobel Kuhn, *In the Arena* (Singapore: Overseas Missionary Fellowship [IHQ] Ltd., 1995) chapter 11.

9. Carl F. H. Henry, *The Pacific Garden Mission: A Doorway to Heaven* (Grand Rapids: Zondervan, 1942), 32.

10. Bertha Smith, *Go Home and Tell* (Nashville: Broadman & Holman, 1995), 81–82.

11. Vance Havner, *Playing Marbles with Diamonds* (Grand Rapids, Mich.: Baker Book House, 1995), 97.

12. J. I. Packer, *Knowing God* (Downers Grove, IL: InterVarsity Press, 1973), 103.

Bible Translations Used

Acknowledgments

This book would not have made it to press without the vision, advice, support, and guidance of the following friends, to whom I express my heartfelt admiration and appreciation:

Greg Johnson of Alive Communications

Brian Hampton of Thomas Nelson Publishers

Kyle Olund of Thomas Nelson Publishers

Katrina Polvinen Morgan

The Donelson Fellowship, Nashville, Tennessee

Thanks!

About the Author

Robert J. Morgan is pastor of the Donelson Fellowship in Nashville, Tennessee, where he has served for more than twenty years. He is the author of ten books including *On This Day*, *Tiny Talks with God*, and *From This Verse*. His *Children's Daily Devotional Bible* won a Gold Medallion Award in 1997. Morgan is an annual lecturer at Fackelbärana, the Torchbearer's School in Holsybrunn, Sweden. He is also a frequent speaker at Christian colleges, conferences, workshops, seminars, and churches. Morgan and his wife, Katrina, have three daughters. Rob is available for speaking engagements and may be contacted through his Web site at www.robertjmorgan.com.